The West Bank Palestinian Family

The West Bank Palestinian Family

Ibrahim Wade Ata

KPI

LONDON, NEW YORK, SYDNEY and HENLEY

First published in 1986 by KPI Limited
11 New Fetter Lane, London EC4P 4EE, England

Distributed by
Routledge & Kegan Paul plc
11 New Fetter Lane, London EC4P 4EE, England

Routledge & Kegan Paul Inc
29 West 35th Street, New York NY 10001

Routledge & Kegan Paul
c/o Methuen Law Book Company
44 Waterloo Road
North Ryde, NSW 2113
Australia

Routledge & Kegan Paul plc
Broadway House, Newtown Road,
Henley-on-Thames, Oxon RG9 1EN, England

Produced by Worts-Power Associates
Set in Times by Typesetters (Birmingham) Limited
and printed in Great Britain
by Short Run Press Ltd., Exeter, Devon.

ISBN 07103 0186 3

Acknowledgements

It is more than polite rhetoric on the writer's part to express a few words of gratitude to a number of individuals and institutions; without their help this work would not have been completed.

As regards individuals, I wish to acknowledge the useful discussions and inspirations of Dr. Sherif Kanaana, president of Al-Najah University, Dr. Emanual Aziz, Dr. Halil Gopur of Yarmouk University, and Dr. Roger Owen of Oxford University.

I am equally grateful to both Brother Eric Vogel, Director of the Computer Centre at Bethlehem University; and Dr. Yilmaz Esmer, Director of the Computer Centre at Boghzichi University, Istanbul. They have spent numerous hours acquainting me with computer analysis and statistical evaluation; their constant critical remarks contributed to shaping my perspective on a number of issues. My thanks also go to Prof. Hisham Sharabi, Dr. George Abed, Dr. M. Masalha, Dr. Victor Billeh, Dr. Adnan Bakheet, Hon. Judge Fu'ad Khoury, Dr. Baramki of Bir Zeit University, Dr. Irwin Hermann, Dr. Adnan El-Amad, Dr. Ali Zaghal, Dr. Bernard Sabella, and especially Dr. Adnan Badran, President of Yarmouk University; their continual encouragement and moral boost will be remembered for a long time. My sincere thanks to Khalil Mosa, Norma Masriyyeh, Michael Howley, and Nihaya Iseed for their technical assistance.

Here I must emphasise that without the assistance of the Jordanian Ministry of National Planning and Development, this work would never have materialised. I also wish to acknowledge the support of the League of Arab States office in London, the Arab Studies Society in East Jerusalem, and the APEF in Washington.

My final word of sincere appreciation to the sociology graduates of 1983 from Bir Zeit University who persevered tremendous legal, political and administrative strain during their administration of this survey.

This work was prepared for and supported by Yarmouk University and the Ministry of National Planning and Development in Jordan.

A Note About Difficulties

The reader should realize that a survey of this nature can only be carried out in the occupied West Bank (and Gaza) under tremendous difficulties not normally faced by a social scientist. Intervening variables, such as the effects of military force(s) and occupation on the life, sanity (or otherwise), and relationships amongst members of the Palestinian family, could not be taken into account. Several questions which should have been included were omitted on the grounds that their inclusion would have jeopardized the whole study. As it was, seventy-five completed questionnaires were confiscated from one interviewer, thus reducing the sample of our study from 1000 down to 925. Another interviewer was interrogated at gunpoint before being turned away from a refugee camp without being able to complete his survey.

Encountering curfews, road checkpoints and travel restrictions within the West Bank was an integral part of this study. It is because the instances encountered are too involved and detailed that we are forced to limit our analysis to the survey findings. Nevertheless, why Palestinian residents of the West Bank, including those who hold Western passports, must strip naked every time they are allowed to re-enter their country of birth is a question beyond our understanding, wit and humanity.

Though this work has been hindered by a few individuals and institutions, I am most grateful to the great majority of participants in this study, who gave unstintingly, both time and advice, to enable me to complete this study.

I wish to dedicate this work to my wife and family, Dani Petocz (1956–1984), and to the Palestinian family on the occupied West Bank for their endurance and sacrifice.

Contents

List of Tables

Appendix

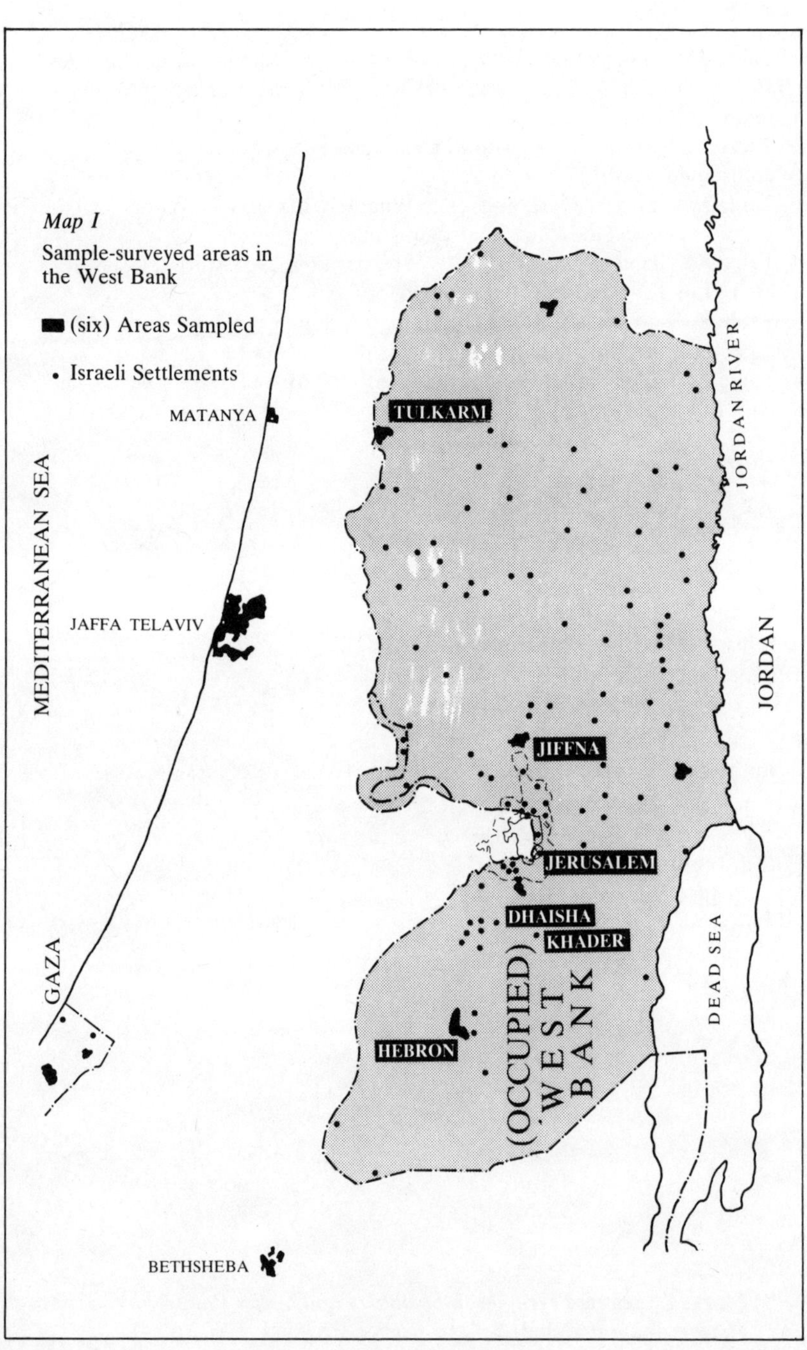

Map I
Sample-surveyed areas in the West Bank
(six) Areas Sampled
Israeli Settlements
MATANYA
TULKARM
MEDITERRANEAN SEA
JAFFA TELAVIV
JORDAN RIVER
JORDAN
JIFFNA
JERUSALEM
DHAISHA
KHADER
(OCCUPIED) WEST BANK
DEAD SEA
GAZA
HEBRON
BETHSHEBA

Chapter 1

Introduction

No doubt the institutions of the family, kinship and marriage form the structural basis of any effective ongoing, dynamic society.

These institutions have a direct effect on the socialising, mental, behavioural and ethical patterns which the family employs. It also regulates social relations between individuals and groups and brings about features which distinguish one family from another and between one society and another.

Being part of a greater society with varying relationships with many social institutions, such as the school, the family transmits whatever changes it encounters during its evolution in the society. Likewise, the repercussions of any changes which affect the society ultimately find their way to the family.

It has become clear that, despite the differing perspectives which socio-anthropological studies have taken regarding the family, a give-and-take relationship continues to exist. The functional theory, for example, attempts to study the way family roles function in the society. The Marxist dialectic theory maintains that the family as a basic unit of the society is influenced by the social and economic changes that affect the society as a whole.[1]

The structural theory, on the other hand, stresses the logical symbioses of the family as an institution, and those which are political, economic and religious. It also examines the way that social roles of members of the family merge with religions,

[1] Marx, K. *Selected Writings in Sociology and Social Philosophy*, ed. by Bottomore and Rubel, Pelican Books, England, 1967 (p.84).

economic and political roles.[2] The interdependence amongst these roles is so strong that one will not understand the family without understanding the functions and nature of its interactions with other institutions. As is illustrated in a later chapter, an economic institution that is being affected by increasing unemployment can make the dependence of hard-stricken classes on their kin much stronger.

Recent literature abounds with studies on the importance of the previously mentioned factors on the family in the Arab Middle East; usually considered reliable and comprehensive sources of reference. Those which tended to focus on marital issues, including the status of women and the segregation of the sexes, have been uniform in their methodology-free approach and content. Yet topics related to the Palestinian family have been virtually ignored and thinly-cultivated to undervalue tremendous political, demographic and social upheavals. Published information on family dynamics, for example, is very scanty and uneven.[3] For example, whilst studies on economic trends and political structures are on the increase, very little has been written on the following areas:

a) Socio-marital changes affecting the Palestinian women which are inconsistent with their traditional role.

b) Marital features which have remained constant and those which have been altered.

c) Changes and adjustments initiated by the Palestinian family in response to socio-political changes in the society at large.

In reading this study, one should bear in mind the purpose and perspective which determined its form and character.

During the early stages of the study, the main focus was intended to be to identify what changes, if any, has the Palestinian family undergone during three generations of its evolution, part of which has taken place under the Israeli occupation since 1967. Either the family has evolved at a natural pace despite the intervening force, or, as a result of the occupation, certain aspects of its development have been speeded up, whilst others have regressed

[2] Parsons, T. and Shils, E. *Toward a General Theory of Action*. Cambridge, Harvard Press, 1952 (p.349).

[3] The first pioneering work on the traditional role of Palestinian women is Hilma Granqvist's *Marriage Conditions in a Palestinian Village, 1931*.

or remained in a state of stalemate.

It was natural to attempt to identify facets of development which the family underwent alongside the remainder of the society. The sample was thus selected from various urban areas, such as towns, villages and refugee camps, in order to determine any possible consistencies and variations. The best way to control whatever regularities, or otherwise, were exhibited in these areas was to divide the area sub-samples into three uniform age groups.

Having set this standard it was then possible to observe who is changing, what is changing, at what rate, in what direction and the differences and uniformities amongst the three generations.

This study presents the reader with the first comprehensive study of the evolution of the Palestinian family in the West Bank of Jordan. The study is intended to examine the following:

a) To gauge the rate of social change in terms of,
   - i the division of labour between the spouses,
   - ii the marital decision-making,
   - iii the family-role enactment,
   - iv the compatibility in attitudes.

b) To examine the salient features and marital inter-relationships within the Palestinian community, and thus to be able to speculate about its future.

c) To find out whether changes which accompany ageing manifest themselves equally amongst towns, villages and camps, and, to a lesser extent, between spouses.

The presentation of sociopsychological data was necessitated by the weight of attitudinal indices in the survey, which is interpreted and presented in an analytical framework. Though the survey was primarily directed towards unbiased analyses of the results obtained, generalisations and speculations on areas where no research has been done, especially since Granqvist's work,[4] became inevitable.

Yet, despite the limitations alluded to, as well as the legal, political and administrative problems as noted in a later chapter, the information gathered should provide social scientists with wide-ranging indices which can be used as a base-line for comparative purposes.

4 *Op. cit.*

The Theoretical Framework of the Study

The study is neither totally based on a hypothetical structure, nor is it presented from an entirely statistical viewpoint.

The temptation to advance theoretical premises without regard to all the circumstances surrounding the study would have tended to unduly influence analysis of the statistical results, as well as the interpretation of certain trends and patterns of the sample.[5]

On the other hand, constructing research on the basis of the statistical findings is quite meaningless and difficult to interpret. Without a contextual framework that enables examination of the problems under examination, the study could well be considered incomplete.

> "We may suddenly realise that some particular past event might have initiated some process whose dynamics we wish to explore, or that the description of the values or climate of opinion during some previous interval might have permitted a test of such psychological forces in initiating the social changes we now experience."[6]

In addition, as regards political, religious and psychological features such as discrimination, identification and national identity, measurements were sometimes inconclusive.

In view of these limitations, it was necessary to devise a concept for the thesis which would accommodate the two approaches. Thus, we have set out to interpret survey results within the context of the family structure on the basis that they can be seen as a direct extension of the Palestinian society. In so doing, we have allowed the possibility of observing the relationship between present circumstances and past determinants.[7]

Our conclusion with social and historical background literature can also be considered justified. The reader should be able to observe the intertwining of empirical and theoretical threads throughout the research.

5 Hyman, H. H. *Secondary Analysis of Sample Surveys*. New York, 1972 (p.11). See also Hagwood, M. and Price, D. *Statistics for Sociologists*. New York, 1952 (pp. 250–296); Siegel, S. *Non-Parametric Statistics for the Behavioural Science*. New York, 1956.

6 Hyman, H. H., *op. cit.* (p.11).

7 See p. 249 in M. Komarovsky's *Common Frontiers of Social Science*, New York, 1957.

Chapter 2

Political and Socio-economic Environment

Introduction

It has been repeatedly pointed out that change in most Arab communities has brought with it disintegration of rigid family structures and led to new modes of living. Different aspects of family life and members of the family, however, may be influenced in different ways and to different degrees. The problem, looked at against the background of the Middle East's traditional family, is to see how the position of the woman is being affected by forces of change, how she is reacting, how different is her social role from the man's and where she is making progress, where the older and younger generations stand on the continuum of change and finally, how they feel as they look towards the future.[1]

It must be admitted at the outset, however, that anyone who presumes to analyse the changing forces at work in regard to the Arab family is treading on precarious ground. Our lack of knowledge about this area's past, coupled with the difficulty of assessing any information on the traditional medievalism of the Palestinian society, leads to difficulties.[2]

Increasingly, one finds reference to the evolution of the family,

[1] Ata, I. 'Prospects and retrospects on the role of Moslem Arab women at present: trends and tendencies' in *Islamic Culture*, Vol. LV, no. 4, 1981.

[2] *ibid.*

including the emancipation of women, as being basically a product of the economic development and the process of industrialisation.[3] Implied in a broad ranging social change, therefore, is the opening of new opportunities for women in the social, economic and political spheres and beyond the domestic life. In short, 'social change fosters the development of alterations to the traditional wife-and-mother role and encourages the taking of attributes that are newly appropriate to the changing society'.[4]

Components of 'modern' societies are synonymous with those of the process of industrialisation.[5] This point is collaborated by Appelbaum, who believes that modernisation theories are uniform in what they propose, namely, that most societies witness uniform sequences of change through the process of industrialisation.[6]

The importance of this observation is that modernisation is synonymous with 'Westernisation' and that most societies will acquire characteristics at the end of modernisation that are similar to those in Western industrialised societies.

A few social scientists disagree with Appelbaum's views on modernisation. In his study of an Arab village, Gullick illustrates that industrialisation does not necessarily bring about uniform features amongst different cultures. For example, although the majority of villagers expressed a great desire in education, they continue to look down on manual and technical work.[7]

It would be relevant to observe that the extended family, a very basic cultural unit, is a concept that goes counter to individuality, competition and social and geographical mobility, all features of industrialisation.

There is a large amount of literature that has focused on the effects of modernisation on the structure of the extended family. The conclusion has not been that there was a change in the character of the latter as a result of the former, but that the two are diametrically opposite.[8] A case in point is Rosenfeld's study of an

3 Goode, W. *World Revolution and Family Patterns*, New York, 1970 (first chapter).

4 Fox, G. 'Some determinants of modernism among women in Ankara', *J.M.F.* Vol. 35, 1975 (p.520).

5 Appelbaum, R. *Theories of Social Change*, Chicago, 1970 (p.36).

6 *ibid*.

7 Gullick, J. 'Old values and new institutions in a Lebanese Arab city', in *Human Organisation*, Vol. 24, no. 1, 1965 (pp.49–52).

8 Kannaná, Sharif, *Change and Continuity* (in Arabic) Jerusalem, Arab Studies Society, 1982.

Arab village inside Israel in 1958. He observed an acceleration in the breaking down of the Palestinian extended family into smaller units as a result of culture contact with the Israeli society.[9]

A second study, on another Palestinian village less than a hundred miles to the north, found, however, that the extended family remains structurally and functionally cohesive despite geographical separation amongst its members. It would also be relevant to mention that the introduction of industry into the village was the reason behind a physical separation between members of the family.[10] The researchers speculate that because of the strong cohesion it was possible for members of the family to become receptive to occupational (and ethical and economic) changes.

The evolution and transformation of the family on the West Bank of Jordan is part of an overall process of change into a disruptive form of existence during the last few decades. Changes in the characteristics of the family have been the result of political, religious, socio-economic and educational forces at work. The weakened authority of Moslem religious leaders, for example, and their reduced power in religious courts since 1967, prevented them from attending to psycho-social problems – the moral forces were suddenly replaced by a vacuum.

Kinship, Structure and Organisation: retrospectives

The most durable of all social institutions is the family. Among many of its functions, ranks high the socialisation of younger members. This, however, did not prevent it from being a changing institution, for, like other social units, it is directly influenced by economic, political, ecological and many other forces inside the society.

Clearly, the structure of the Palestinian family is intertwined with, and ultimately is influenced by, other structures in the society.

Until recently the Palestinian Arab community has been under

9 Rosenfeld, H. 'Process of structural change within the Arab-village extended family' *American Anthropology*, Vol. 60 (pp.1127–1139).

10 Williams, H. and Williams, J. 'The extended family as a vehicle of cultural change' *Human Organisation*, Vol. 24 (pp.59–64).

similar societal influences to those of many Arab countries. Rights and obligations of both sexes have, for example, altered little from the norm of other Arab communities.

In urban Palestine, what existed between the 10th and the 19th centuries is basically a patriarchal type of society, in which the extended family was ritualistically governed by Islam, but was operating to cultural and social imperatives. In that sense, the Christian family differed only marginally in character from the mainstream of the community.

The Palestinian Arab family displayed many features that existed in complex traditional societies. Chief amongst them was the dependence of the individual on his family and his integration into it in such an intense way that the Palestinian culture was rightly termed 'a kinship culture'[11]; and, in order to maintain cohesion and solidarity among family members, marriage was arranged by its elders. The newly-wedded couple were to live in the household of the bridegroom's father as were their children and grandchildren.

Power and authority were distributed according to age and sex. Elderly males, as a consequence, espoused the highest form of authority status, dependency and repression. At the same time, women were to observe prescribed roles and obligations. Amongst these obligations were obedience and care of children.

These observations are not intended to present the reader with a bleak image of the family. On the contrary, the traditional extended family did provide its members with economic and social security amongst many other advantages, as one will see later.

One of the many duties of the extended family is finding employment for its needy members. The Arabic term for this kind of duty is *wastah*, or a go-between (the needy and the employer). Like any other Arab society, but perhaps to a lesser extent, the Palestinian society resorts to such a practice so that one is not cheated in the market place, in locating and acquiring a job, in resolving conflict and legal litigation, in winning a court decision, in speeding a government action, in establishing and maintaining political influence or bureaucratic procedures, in finding a bride and, in fact, for the social scientist to locate and convince respon-

[11] Othman, A. and Redfield, R. 'An Arab view of point IV'. The University of Chicago Round Table No. 749, August 3rd 1952.

dents to give an interview.[12]

The *hamayel* system, or the combination of families, headed by a representative of the most powerful and elitist family, continued throughout the British system. The lineage heads are today, by and large, accountable through delegation of duties to the Israeli military regime. Through favouritism and paternalism it upholds and relegates the traditional structure of the village, in social functions, administrative matters and allocation of certain occupational duties. It is true, however, that the so-called village league heads are isolated from a large section of the community; they derived much of their power from the military occupation.

Such a grouping of members of a kin group was so essential in its support of the individual, and in turn in his allegiance to it if he wanted to ensure his economic and political survival. Membership of one's kin group eventually delineated specific performances, rights and obligations.

It was natural that this kind of socio-economic differentiation raised certain sub-systems, or 'societies', which aimed at servicing the individual's welfare as long as he was a member of a certain kin group or sect. Such charity-oriented societies continue to function in most villages, camps or towns throughout the West Bank. The Y.M.C.A.[13] in Jerusalem is a fitting example here. Though Christian in name, it is not affiliated to any sect, government agency or foreign institution. One of its aims has been to provide opportunities to transcend kinship-oriented communities. Though its appeal is mainly confirmed to sports activities at present, its overall success is the subject of an independent study.

Farsoun believes that the kinship organisation throughout the Arab world remained basically the same, and continued, particularly during the British mandate, to be quite strong. He notes,

> "industrialisation hardly made serious inroads; the economic base remained largely just above self-sufficiency in rural agrarian villages, and mercantilistic in urban centres – types for which cohesive extended family relations are very well-suited. Given the paucity of resources and of work, the

12 Farsoun, S. in Sweet, L. ed. *op. cit.*, 1970 (p.70). See also Ayoub, V. 'Conflict resolution and social reorganisation in a Lebanese village' in *Human Organisation*, Vol. 24, Spring 1965 (p.13).

13 Otherwise known as Young Men's Christian Association.

> extended family, both in rural and urban areas, remained the major institution for guaranteeing the survival and happiness of the individual human. Political, religious, educational and welfare structures all contributed to and reinforced this kinship organisation."[14]

The traditional image of the Palestinian family during the twentieth century did witness breakthrough changes in some aspects of its character. New modes of communication, media exposure, co-educational universities and Western missionary schools, as well as education and urbanisation, have loosened the bonds of old social mores on the family.

In the same instance, the Western model of modernisation is clearly dysfunctional if it is applied to the Palestinian community on the West Bank. The sequence of the model is outlined as follows: increased urbanisation raises literacy levels, which in turn expand media exposure; an increase in media exposure leads to a wider participation in both the economic and political life.[15]

Given the obvious interference by the Israeli occupational forces in the political and economic institutions of the West Bank, the sequence of events outlined earlier no longer applies.[16]

The four stage sequence is an essential requirement to move away from an isolated, traditional way of life in the direction of modernisation. The underlying assumption is one whereby the individual assumes a psycho-physical mobility – an intrinsic step towards social change.

A precise definition of the above is in order. Mobile individuals are those who have the opportunity to attain new sets of skills notwithstanding a change of environment in order to change their future:[17]

> "A mobile society (according to Lerner) has to encourage rationality. For the calculus of choice shapes individual behaviour and conditions its rewards. People came to see the social future as manipulable rather than ordained, and their

[14] Farsoun, S. in Sweet, L. ed., *op. cit.* (p.260).
[15] Lerner, D. *The Passing of Traditional Society* (p.48).
[16] Zureik, E. and Nakhle, K. *ed., Sociology of the Palestinians*, London, Groom Helm, 1980.
[17] Lerner, D. *op. cit.* (pp.48–49).

personal prospects in terms of achievement rather than heritage."[18]

Religious and Socio-economic Organisation

The character of the Palestinian Society on the West Bank resembles to a large extent the character of its Lebanese counterpart. Since the Ottoman rule it has been composed of religiously and urbanly diverse, ethnically varied, mainly complex, semi-agrarian entities. The main difference being that the modern Lebanese constitution was formulated in 1943 to accommodate the various ethnic, religious and political communities.

Given the religious urban social diversity it should be assumed that what is true of inhabitants of one place will not always apply with respect to those of another. Observations of differences in the subject areas under investigation between Christians and Moslems, town, village and camp dwellers will be made whenever possible. It is of particular interest to observe that very few researchers have so far examined the Moslem–Christian interrelationship within the Palestinian community. At the same time, throughout the centuries, affiliates of different sects and inhabitants of different settlements on the West Bank have undergone a remarkably uniform experience such as that during the past 16 years.

On the West Bank, as it is in most of the Arab societies, there is no separation between Church (and I use the word here to apply to both Moslem and Christian institutions) and State (and I mean here the occupied territory, including East Jerusalem). The influence of religion on most aspects of one's life is obvious, including matters such as divorce, baptism, courtship, death and marriage. Civil marriage, for example, is something that is not heard of, let alone accepted. Likewise, inter-marriage is still a very rare occurrence.[19] In addition, one's own entity is/has been intertwined with one's sectarian affiliation. Unlike most other cultures in the whole of the Middle East religion is an obligation, not a preference. Indeed, it was no surprise to note that there was an

[18] *ibid.* (p.48).

[19] Only two cases of inter-marriage were observed in the survey sample covering 925 households.

absolutely complete sample response indicating sectarian affiliation.

The most important instrument through which religion exercised its hold on the individual was the traditional partriarchal extended family. As the family system was supported by religion, being a religious institution, family and religion eventually supported each other. When the individual left his family behind, he had rejected an inately religious atmosphere.[20]

Christian missionary schools have had certain influences, peripheral as they may be, on the decline of parental authority, a loosening up of family control and an initiation of Western family structures and social reforms.[21]

Christian schools on the West Bank, be they French, German, Swedish, English, American or Italian, if not totally administered directly by respective foreign administration, would be dependent on funds from these governments or private institutions.

It has become clear that, just as a Palestinian individual is expected to be identified with a wide-ranging kinship, the same applies with a particular sect. For, if the latter is not fulfilled his identity would neither be considered complete nor accepted.

The Socio-economic Structure and the Israeli Presence

The victory of the Israeli military in the first Arab–Israeli war in 1948 resulted in 900,000 Palestinians seeking refuge in camps distributed over a number of Arab countries, including the West Bank region.[22]

Nineteen years later another exodus, totalling 200,000, headed towards East Jordan as a result of the Six Day War in 1967. (Although the West Bank has remained under occupation for almost 17 years, it is still legally tied to East Jordan according to international laws and the Jordanian constitution.)

The demographic composition of refugees varies slightly

[20] Ata, I. 'Impact of westernising and other factors on the changing status of Moslem women', (forthcoming in *Eastern Anthropologist* Vol. 37, (2), 1984 (pp.95–126).

[21] *ibid.*

[22] Hopkins, N. 'The evolution of Palestinian Arab society' in S. Ibrahim *ed. Arab Society in Transition* (pp.246–7).

between one specialised study and another. The majority of studies, such as that of Asfour,[23] estimated that 80% of the population of camp refugees in 1956 was composed of women and children; the remainder were predominantly unskilled male farmers.

Though it is not the focus of this study to analyse the reasons behind the Palestinian exodus, a reference to the actual determinants can shed some light on how the beliefs and social values, which Palestinian refugees brought with them from the towns and villages have been uniformly transplanted in their newly-set camps.[24] For example, Dodd and Barakat found in their study in 1968 that fear of dishonouring of the family by Israeli soldiers' threats was the primary factor behind their plight.[25]

Other social values, such as family dignity and cohesion, role of women, respect for the aged could have only served to reinforce the traditional village social infrastructure.

In the same way, migration from villages to settled areas brought with it rural socio-cultural and demographic norms. Of these we select life expectancy, birth and death rates, levels of fertility, educational levels and health awareness.

This does not mean, however, a total restructuring of the social and family life in the resettled areas as this naturally depends on the level of contact and integration between the two communities. A case in point relates to the Egyptian rural migration trends where fertility norms, for instance, tended to linger in largely unassimilated urban fringe areas.[26]

Changes in the patterns of the economic system were felt soon after the occupation of the West Bank in 1967, by the Israeli army. The effects of the altered economy gradually filtered down to social and cultural facets in the community. Indeed, the subjection of the economy of the West Bank to the economic order of Israel was nowhere stronger than for the East Jerusalem residents.[27]

[23] Asfour, E. 'The economic framework of the Palestine problem' in Polk, W., *et. al. Backdrop to Tragedy*. Boston, Beacon Press, pp.307–364 (p.340).

[24] Sirhan, B. 'Palestinian refugee camp life in Lebanon.' *J.P.S.* Vol. 4, (2), 1975 (pp.91–107).

[25] Dodd, P. and Barakat, H. *River without Bridges*. Beirut, I.P.S. 1968.

[26] Abu-Lughod, J. 'Migrant adjustment of city life – the Egyptian case' *American Journal of Sociology* Vol. 67, 1961–62 (p.22).

[27] See the end of the chapter for a detailed analysis.

The overall economic changes were in favour of unskilled workers as a result of labour shortage and an increasing demand for workers inside Israel. Not surprisingly, members of the same household became effective wage earners. In fact, for the first time, the Palestinian community witnessed the rise of the lower (and rural) classes who began to enjoy financial prosperity. This eventually led to a heightened change in self-evaluation, prestige and status, even though Heller[28] contends that the status of the 'hierarchy' remained generally coherent. For example, rather than abandoning their traditionally prestigious jobs, teachers began supplementing their income with some additional employment. Merchants, on the other hand, have enjoyed increasing profits, being the sole agents of food items that were exported from Jordan but were replaced by Israeli products.

The surplus value which was created by the Israeli economy was satisfied by cheap labour. This was most noticeable with regard to women. As Hopkins elaborates:

> "the most exploited segment of this (cheap) labour is the women who work in the textile and food processing industries for lower wages than men. At home, the wages of working daughters are often taken by fathers to provide the cash needed to support higher levels of consumption. At the other end of the scale, some families have become migrant farm labourers, frequenting Israeli farm settlements; this allows the Palestinian woman to work for cash on the farms while continuing to look after her family".[29]

Before 1967 there were almost no movements between village and city amongst workers. There was, however, mass migration of male workers, skilled and non-skilled, to the Arab Gulf nations during the early sixties to earn a better living in the shortest time possible. Leaving the wife behind as the second-in-charge must have produced different effects on patterns of socialisation and child-rearing practices. The influence of migration on the social structure and the family is a subject of many studies. Migration and economics are closely linked, for example, in the sense that attachment of children of emigrés to their home country and

[28] Heller, M. in Migdal, J. (1980) *ed. op. cit.* (p.196).

[29] Hopkins, N. 'The evolution of the Palestinian Arab society' in S. Ibrahim, *ed.* (p.432).

kinship is much weaker.[30] Add to that the strength of inter-relationship between the labour force and emigration of workers which often leads to unequal distribution in occupational categories. A detailed consideration of the psychosocial repercussions does warrant a totally separate and devoted study.

Yet, 1967 was a year that marked a revolutionary change for West Bank villagers seeking work outside their place of residence. The movement expanded greatly in time and now forms a permanent feature in the Israeli economy. The latest estimates have the figure of Arab labourers who work in the Israeli economy at 80,000.[31] Such patterns of employment no doubt swayed many peasants away from the agricultural land in the direction of relatively high-paid unskilled wage labour.[32]

Many reasons lie behind this lifting pattern. The primary one is that the Arab agricultural sector lags immensely behind the Israeli one. An Arab who is employed in the Israeli agricultural system earns twice as much as one who works within the Arab system.[33]

In 1973 the West Bank ranked third, next to Israel and the United States, in absorbing exported items from the Israeli market. By the late 1970s the West Bank and Gaza Strip became the largest consuming market, thus absorbing 25% of Israel's total exports.[34] The invasion of highly-inflated Israeli products, including highly-taxed bread and butter items, in West Bank markets placed additional strains on the Palestinian family.

The domination of the Israeli economic system namely, wage labour, brought about numerous changes in the social structure of the urban community.

30 Lauer, R. H. *Perspectives on Social Change*. Boston, Allwyn and Bacon Inc., 1977 (pp.4–6).

31 *Central Bureau of Statistics* (1978) 'Employed persons from Judaea, Samaria, and the Gaza Strip working in Israel, April–June 1977. *QSAT*, Vol. 8, No. 2, Jerusalem, October 1978 (Hebrew); see also 1983 report.

32 A relevant table showing the extent to which features of the traditional employment in the sample have changed can be found in a later chapter on demographic features.

33 Rosenfeld, H. 'Farm peasantry to wage labour and residential peasantry: the transformation of an Arab village' in Sweet, L. *ed.* (p.167).

34 Extracted from the *Statistical Abstract of Israel* (1977) (pp.36, 37, 195).

Firstly, the demand for unskilled and manual workers in the Israeli industry evened out the salary distribution across various classes. The white collar classes – a case in point – gave away their Jordanian civil service jobs to Israeli employees. This accelerated the emigration of ex-civil servants and the educational classes – alongside the bourgeois land owners from Jerusalem, Ramallah and Bethlehem whose land became confiscated[35] into Western and neighbouring Arab countries.[36]

The Altered Status of East Jerusalem

Historically speaking, Arab (East) Jerusalem was separated from the remainder of the city and was placed under the Jordanian authority in 1948. Thus, in 1967, when Israel occupied the Arab part of the city it decided to annex it forcibly into the Jewish identity.

The planning of Arab East Jerusalem was peripheral to that of the western-orientated Jewish part. Not only was the planning different, but it was second in importance and interest to the Jewish side. For example 20,000 Palestinians were expelled from East Jerusalem on the pretext of lack of space, whilst at the same time 5,000 Jews took their place.[37]

The emphasis on a Western style of urban planning had polarised the two communities physically, architecturally and psychologically. Dakkak observes that East Jerusalem became a place to be visited whilst the Western side be worked at and lived in.[38] The emphasis of the archaeological enshrinement of the Eastern side of Jerusalem made the Palestinian become aware of the Zionist policy of disregarding him and his habitat as a living

35 In 1980 the figure is put at 20,000 under confiscation in the Jerusalem region. This figure is observed, however, to change with time; see Stock, E. and Mansour, A., 'Arab Jerusalem after annexation', *New Outlook* Vol. 14, No. 1, Jan 1971 (pp.28–33).

36 Abu–Lughod, I. *ed. The Transformation of Palestine*, Evanston, 111, 1971; Abu Ayyash, A.I. 'Israeli settlement policy in the West Bank and Gaza Strip', *Samed al. Iqtisadi*, Vol. 4, No. 31, August 1981 (pp.75–98) (in Arabic).

37 Sharon, A. *Planning Jerusalem the Old City and its Environs*, Jerusalem, Weidenfeld and Nicholson, 1973 (pp.159–177).

38 Dakkak, I. 'Jerusalem via Dolorosa', *Journal of Palestine Studies* Vol. XI, No. 1, Autumn 1981 (pp.139–41).

potential. The dilemma became exaggerated as he (the Palestinian) obtained:

> "an identity card which enables him to reside in Israel and gives him the right to take part in local (but not parliamentary) elections and the right to benefit from his social rights as a resident. He also has a Jordanian passport with all the rights of citizenship involved in holding such a passport.
>
> These are the contradictions the Jerusalemite has to take into account as he decides what is a safe course to steer if he is to avoid coming into collision with the (security) conditions of either party. He anxiously tries to discover a common denominator in the day-to-day conduct of his affairs and has to rely on the indulgence now of the Jordanian, now of the Israeli side."[39]

Such an atmosphere of contradiction is exacerbated as the remainder of the Arab world pressures the Jerusalem community to preserve their identity with a little backing of national institutions to withstand Judaisation of East Jerusalem.

The subjugation of East Jerusalem inhabitants for the first time into Israeli income tax, in the face of a devaluated shekel and the revival of the Jordanian economy, led to the outflow of West Bank capital into banks in Jordan. Subsequently, those who decided against emigration witnessed a decline in their socio-economic status and became better known as the proletariat.[40]

In contrast, skilled workers increased, as did their wages. For example, in 1968 the wage of Palestinian workers formed 3.3% of the National (West Bank) income, whereas by 1978 it had risen to 24.4%.[41] As a result of the creation of the new economic class, which included village peasants, family farms acquired an altered role in the life of the family.[42] Tamari contends that though the farm has not lost its total significance, it has acquired a new subsidiary dimension.[43] The management and control of farms by

[39] *ibid.* (p.141).

[40] Weigert, Gideon *Israeli Presence in East Jerusalem.* Jerusalem, Gideon Weigert, 1973 (pp.64–66).

[41] Van Arkadie, B. *Benefits and Burdens. A Report on the West Bank and Gaza Strip Economics Since 1967.* Washington D.C., Carnegie Endowment for International Peace, 1977 (pp.122–3).

[42] Tamari, S. 'Building other people's home' *Arab Thought Forum*, 1981 (p.31).

[43] *ibid.* (p.62).

kinship members, namely in villages, became a symbol of unity and of functioning as an economic unit. All the same, an incessant confiscation of agricultural land (almost 45% of the West Bank is now confiscated) has begun to place the kinship structure under jeopardy.

The implications of such development are varied. The most relevant is that through the alteration of the socio-economic structure, the *Wajaha*, traditionally a social status associated with land ownership, was eliminated. Duties such as consultation, deputisation and conciliation which traditionally were performed by highly regarded village representatives, were disrupted. The traditional authority of the *Hamula*, including other legal channels in the community, lost ground. In place of the established hierarchy, with its wide-ranging influence on social relations, an authority newly formulated by the Israeli regime so-called the village league, came into effect. Included in their main duties are such matters as offering directions and facilities to sponsor the re-emigration of their refugee relatives in the East Bank.

The urban family is becoming an 'Arab' version of the nuclear family with some alterations, allowing for grown-up children to remain living with their parents until they get married. These alterations will be illustrated later on.

The effects of the occupation on the community, and to a lesser extent Arab workers who have direct contact with Israeli employers and authorities, are tangible. Being the undisputed household heads, males prefer to represent their wives in most dealings with Israeli government officials.

The class identity of Palestinian workers in Israel was observed to have acquired new features which evolved into their character. For example, the relationship between men and women became a little more polarised as a result of the men being exposed to alien ideas and technologically oriented activities. Women were contained in their traditionally based, non-complementary role.

For the first time, many individuals found themselves making independent decisions, thus taking full responsibility for their actions without reference to their kinship or reliance on their immediate relations. Individual plans were made without the total submission to the authority of the household head.[44]

Repercussions of changes to a traditional inbalance of marital

[44] Tamari, S. *op. cit.* (1980) (pp.147–148).

relationships are, of course, not uniform across our research sample, as we shall see in detail in a later chapter.

The repercussions outlined above are not totally confined to the East Jerusalem community; they were felt, though to a lesser extent, in many other West Bank communities. For example, Islamic courts of law were not abrogated, and thus continued to function as arbitrary bodies in family disputations and other civil matters.

References to traditional heritage and religious codes were not a regular practice, as these ceased to be the ultimate source of consultation. The general attitude was one in which the Palestinian community wanted to convince itself that preserving one's heritage is the last resort to maintain social cohesion in political turmoil.[45] Reference to religion in times of crises can only lead to spiritual and psychological comfort.

Advocates of this attitude never attempted to adopt Western values, even those values which could be accommodated in a traditional religious heritage. Their support is believed to be on the increase in the absence of the psychological, social and cultural background.[46]

Changes in Psychosocial Conditions

The psychosocial conditions of the community as a whole have a direct bearing on the structure and dynamics of the family. Likewise, the stability of the community is directly related to the stability of the family. The general psychological distress of any displaced community ultimately reflects feelings of distress, uneasiness and other related syndromes. Relevant to our subject is a study by Shamir on the refugee family in Palestine. He noted that what refugees lacked most was *istiqrar*, which roughly translates into psychosocial stability and feelings of security.[47]

It is generally believed that change is possible, when it is not forced on people, but when they desire it and accept it themselves; that is 'when people want to change rather than merely submit to

45 Escribano, M. *op. cit.* (p.159).
46 Dakkak, I. (pp.142–144).
47 Shamir, S., in Migdal, J. *ed.* (p.149).

change'.[48] If change is, however, only partial it might lead to social uncertainties and disorders.

In the face of total dissatisfaction with the Israeli occupation, the condition for social change is no longer a determining variable to the Palestinian community.

Two other factors have also been noted as significant to overall social change. These are the influences of leaders in the community and the absence of generational factionalism.[49]

Devoting a detailed analysis to the above factors would not be necessary to this study; suffice to note that daily editorials in Arabic papers suggest a minor role for the two factors.

Social change is a thinly stretched concept referring to alterations in social phenomena in varying facets of human life, beginning with the individual and ending with the community.[50] Underlying the definition is the rate and direction of change, and the alteration of all features in social life.

It has already been pointed out that in addition to the disruption of the local economy, other modes of social life have altered, even the manifestations of change was uneven, tentative, ambiguous and often contradictory.[51] The result of an overall exposure to a foreign economy and a foreign culture was in itself a challenge to the indigenous Palestinian culture.

The most obvious of reactions was the overrushed feelings of bewilderment and excitement of anti-traditional outward styles of behaviour such as dress, sexual intimacy and easy-going behaviour of the Israelis in the months which immediately followed the 1967 June War.

The emotional surge was later modified, and in recent years reversed its pace.[52] Shebadeh remarks that all values, norms and beliefs were put to the test and were relatively shaken. Progress and modernity of Jews were viewed as inevitable determinants of

[48] Mead, M., *New Lives for Old*. New York, Mentor Book, 1961 (p.320); also Redfield, R. *A Village That Chose Progress: Chan Kom Revisited*, Chicago, University Press, 1956.

[49] Chance, N. 'Culture change and integration' in *American Anthropologist*, Vol. 62, 1960 (pp.1033–6).

[50] Lauer, R. H. *Perspectives on Social Change*, Boston, Allyn and Bacon, Inc. 1977 (pp.4–6).

[51] Heller, M. in Migdal, J. *ed.* (p.187).

[52] Shehadeh, A. 'The Palestinian demand for peace, justice and an end to bitterness' in *New Middle East*, Vol. 35, Aug. 1971 (p.22).

their victory. The community in a muted manner admire the freedom and individualism of the Israelis, yet its deep-seated tradition tells it that there is something fine about its heritage which should be preserved and cherished.

The general consensus was that there are values in the oriental way of life which must not be jeopardised; virtues such as 'family ties', 'respect for others', 'willingness to sacrifice' must be preserved. Certainly Palestinians in Jerusalem want their children to enjoy the material (and social security) advantages offered to them, but they insist that the Palestinian way of life is still fundamentally the better way. In this respect, the older generation constantly complains about the younger for manners and morals which are changing fairly rapidly. (Change, here, means a general movement towards the Israeli–Western pattern, even when it is charitably called 'modernisation'.)

With regards to intellectuals and university students,[53] their objective has been to change the Palestinian mentality that focused on social and economic needs into controversial issues related to cultural identity under the occupation. (Economic development was considered something beyond repair, since the economic system was being subjected to policies of the occupying power. Also, social change can take place in a politically stable environment.)

The effects of social changes were felt most amongst East Jerusalem families. Conflicts between parents and children became more exacerbated soon after the enforcement of the Israeli law there, and as the Islamic religious hierarchy lost much of its clout over the 'delinquent' social behaviour of the young generation. In fact, for the first time the father was penalised in the Israeli courts of law for inflicting physical harm on his daughter.[54]

Enforced Hebrew curriculum in the schools of East Jerusalem has assisted in making the Israeli culture more accessible to school children. Their exposure and contact with the 'other' culture made them envious of the permissive liberal life-style of the Israeli youth. Resentment of sex role constraints, traditional parental control and lack of freedom must have contributed to a change of

[53] The West Bank currently boasts four universities which are regularly being closed down by the military authorities since they are viewed as the primary Palestinian national hot-beds.

[54] Interview with lawyer Jonathan Kuttab in Jerusalem on 13th December 1982.

thinking and feeling. It has indeed contributed to abandonment of what they see as superfluous aspects of their heritage.

Parents' grievances about their children's lack of respect, disobedience to authority and lack of discipline have become quite common.

In Heller's own words:

> "the challenge obviously does not stem from the inherent attractiveness of Israel. Israel does, however, embody certain Western cultural forms and values that have long inspired sectors of the West Bank population and especially the counter-elite intellectuals and party activists that grew up during the Jordanian periods. In other words, the forces undermining tradition are not specifically Israeli but they are greatly strengthened by the Israeli presence on the West Bank".[55]

Conclusions

This study aims at identifying the features which may alter the structure and dynamics of the family across three generations, as well as those which have withstood forces of change on the West Bank of Jordan. The situation in East Jerusalem is given particular attention because of its altered legal status.

After being annexed to Israel in 1967. Subsequently comparative observations on family characteristics and others between the communities in Jerusalem and the West Bank are occasionally made in the hopes that they will provide more insight and meaning to conclusions reached.

No doubt, the Israeli presence on the West Bank has brought with it changes in economic and social attitudes and aspirations within the community. The precise degree and nature of such changes, for example whether they are real or perceived, whether they are even between the East Jersualem inhabitants and the remainder of the West Bank and whether they are markedly contrasted with the East Bank community is not easy to measure or predict.

The scope of changes that transformed the Palestinian type of

[55] Heller, M. in Migdal, J. *op. cit.* (p.199).

employment, that is, from peasant or small-town life into an Israeli owned, wage-labour economy, must have contributed, however little, to the adopting of new behavioural patterns. This means that whilst they were on the job they accepted direction, wore different clothes, received information in another language and were exposed to different codes of ethics and behaviour.

In addition, changes in the patron–client relationship have also been felt.[56] No longer do workers from lower classes feel dependent, as they have traditionally, on the Jordanian economic elite businessmen, landowners and their organisations. In addition lower class families in East Jerusalem have benefited most from social services.[57]

Influence of the traditional Bourgerise elite has weakened markedly since 1967. Like many self-employed workers and small business traders who were subjected to heavy taxes, they sought relief in migrating overseas.[58]

The 'old' families' loss of their economic and religious prestige created a vacuum amongst the West Bank community, especially in East Jerusalem. In the absence of national institutions and a weakened leadership, socio-cultural and traditional/non-traditional boundaries began to emerge. At first there was a move towards adopting and imitating trappings of a Western(ised) Israeli culture. By law, women in East Jerusalem found that they have equal status and rights to their male counterparts. This, of course, carries with it a subtle message to both men and women in that they must re-evaluate each other, their family values and behaviour, the authority of ancient family tradition and so forth. It has also indirectly resulted in an increasing coolness towards

56 Interview with Palestinian American lawyer, Jonathon Kuttab, 13th December 1983 in East Jerusalem.

57 Kanovsky, E. *The Economic Impact of the Six Day War*. New York, Praeger, 1970 (pp.163–7); Abu Shilbaya, M. 'Jerusalem before and after June: an Arab view.' *New Middle East*, March/April 1972 (pp.42–43). *Al-Rai* newspaper in its edition of 5th February 1984 lists no less than 50 shopkeepers in East Jerusalem who shut down their business because of heavy taxes.

58 Pressures to emigrate were not, however, always economic. The Karp report, drawn up by a Justice Ministry Commission in May 1982 and published in *The Jerusalem Post* on 8th February 1984 after a 20 month delay.

religion as a whole – religion being traditionally considered a total way of life.[59]

During the recent years a national movement whose aim was to reactivate traditional values began to emerge.

The 'reactivation' phenomenon was intensified in order to protect tradition and to control the structural changes which the society was exposed to. Feeling threatened by the Israeli acculturation, many have turned to traditional manifestations, chief amongst them is a return to wearing the religious attire or *Sharia*.

The effects of political forces on the social life of the community was so intense that Western-oriented organisations, such as *The Lions' Club*, were dissolved.

In summary, the Palestinian family is neither in its traditional role nor is it fully liberated in the modern sense. Rather it is in a state of transition, 'one of flux and incongruency', causing individuals to be 'torn by internal conflicts, competing obligations and contradictory expectations'.[60] The Palestinian family manifests great inbalances between duties and rights, aspirations and attainments, espoused values and actual behaviour.[61] Women may have gained some degree of freedom by mixing at universities or working outside, joining national movements of protest, but they are not completely emancipated.

Underlying the diversity of opinions on the subject of worst features of marriage, and in regard to comparisons between post- and pre-1967,[62] is a growth in tensions as if the community is no longer unified in its practices and goals, only in problems. The underlying query being should the 'old' ways give way to the new ones!

Yet, whatever changes occurred since the 1967 occupation, they could not have permeated the inner layers of the Palestinian culture sufficiently to alter the very basis of the structure of the family.

Nowadays tension on the West Bank is generated by enforcing the culture on the Palestinian, and penetrating it through

59 Patai, R. 'Religion in Middle Eastern, Far Eastern and Western Culture', *South Western Journal of Anthropology*, Vol. 10, Autumn 1954 (pp.233–54).

60 Ibrahim, S. E. *Arab Society in Transition*, Cairo, American University, 1977 (p.86).

61 *ibid*. p.86.

62 See tables IV and XV in the Appendix.

dominant modes of communications, television, radio and an altered school curriculum.

The reader must keep in mind that in the light of an intervening variable of occupation it is difficult to develop a systematic theory to explain the dynamics of evolution of the Palestinian family.

Chapter 3

Administration of the Survey

A: Planning and designing of the questionnaire

A structured questionnaire was devised in a manner that would provide an optimum level of information. At first glance, a number of questions may appear repetitious, but this characteristic serves the purpose of extracting the maximum amount of information and gauging the respondent's reliability.

The questionnaire was designed in such a manner that it would determine differences and association between certain attitudinal variables across different age groups and amongst camp refugees, villagers and city dwellers.

The main focus of the questionnaire was on:

(a) Socio-economic changes affecting Palestinian women which are inconsistent with their traditional role. The rate of social change was gauged in terms of:

- *i* division of labour between the spouses,
- *ii* marital decision making,
- *iii* family role enactment.

(b) Marital conditions which have remained constant and those which have altered.

(c) Marital adjustment and the way which it was affected by changes in the society at large. Variables of adjustment included:

- *i* pleasing and displeasing features in marriage,
- *ii* problems and tensions compared to pre-1967 conditions,
- *iii* uniformity of interest, compromising decisions etc.

The major difficulty in designing the questionnaire was the unavailability of research on the Palestinian family which could have provided concrete foundations for formulating hypotheses.

The method of 'personal interview' was adopted because of the compelling advantages it enjoys in data collection over other methods.[1]

Firstly, in creating a pleasant and relaxed atmosphere one is able to develop the interviewee's interest and arouse his curiosity in the survey.[2] A face to face approach was decided to be preferable to other methods with the community under analysis, in that it permits a greater flexibility in clarifying questions and answers. The inability of the respondents to recognise the subtle differences in 'multiple-choice' answers in Arabic was common. The rigid semantic structure of semitic languages was probably the foundation of this difficulty. The interviewer is then in a position of being able to obtain a reasonably unbiased picture of the reactions, spontaneity, life-style and level of comprehension of the respondents. The not insignificant ratio of illiterates[3] was a further justification for this approach.

As many as 68% of the sample, for example, found it difficult to distinguish the differences between the phrases strongly agree, agree, indifferent, disagree and strongly disagree. During an interview in the pilot study, the respondent stated 'there is only right or wrong, yes or no, you either know how to swim or you don't'. Subsequently, questions of this kind were eliminated. Because the questionnaire was designed for persons who were expected to have a low level of education, the vocabulary was selected with extreme care and simplicity. In doing so it was hoped that unnecessary ambiguity and elaboration were eliminated.

The main empirical problem in dealing with questions of change was the absence of longitudinal data; that is, the inability to establish progressive cut-off points. A better way would be to collect data from the sample at different times in their life-cycle. In the absence of the former an approximation of generational change can be obtained by comparing responses of different age-

1 See also, Lininger, C. A., *et. al. The Sample Survey: Theory and Practice*. New York, McGraw Hill, 1975 (p.128); Kish, L. *Survey Sampling*. New York, Wiley, 1965; Hyman, H. H. *Survey Design and Analysis*, New York, Free Press, 1955.

2 *ibid*. (p.129).

3 See Table XI, Chapter 4.

categories. Accordingly, the sample was divided into three age groups and then responses were compared according to selected attitudes and behaviour patterns.

B: Methodology and Research Problems

A sample size of 1200 households was set as a target for the survey research. The number, though it could be considered small for an elaborate and comprehensive study, was chosen as being sufficiently flexible to permit statistical reliability, as well as measurement of mean scores of variables of groups under examination. The other determinants that prompted our sample size were that a thousand households was too large a sample for field work of three months duration to be carried out whilst the author was on one term secondment from his university in East Jordan; the widespread nature of the areas in which the respondents were living; the difficulties of conducting the survey at night and so on. The latter factor is of a particular concern to us because of military road blocks, curfews and, occasionally during day time, widespread arrests by the Israeli military.

The survey sample was sorted out from three primary milieux reflecting variations in the Palestinian life, namely city inhabitants, town dwellers and camp refugees. The two cities were East Jerusalem and Hebron, the villages were Khader and Jiffna and the two refugee camps were Dhaisha and Tul-Karem. The six areas were selected because of the geographical, religious and population distribution.

East Jerusalem is the most urbane and highly exposed to Western and Israeli cultures of Arab city areas; it has a large number of restaurants, missionary schools, international hotels, a radio station, four regularly published papers and is roughly equally divided between Moslems and Christians. By contrast, Hebron has no theatres, no hotels or restaurants and is basically Moslem and conservative. Each of the two cities is populated by approximately 100,000 inhabitants.

East Jerusalem is of unique interest as it was forcibly annexed by Israel. For example, Israel began moving its government offices to East Jerusalem as if it were the sovereign power in the city, transforming its demographic and physical features and historic character. Though Abba Eban, Israel's representative to the

U.N., declared to the General Assembly that 'the legal status of Jerusalem is different from the territory in which Israel is sovereign', Israel passed a law on 30th July 1980 which made Jerusalem its *de jure* capital. As such, papers published in (Arab) East Jerusalem, by law, are not to be distributed to Palestinians who live on the West Bank.

East Jerusalem holds a special place among cities of the world because Christians, Moslems and Jews all regard it as a spiritual centre. For this reason, Jerusalem has been historically controlled by religious communities who resided in the ancient quarters of the city and oversaw their Holy Places.

Jiffna was selected because it is predominantly Christian and is situated in the northern section of the West Bank. Khader was selected because it is predominantly Moslem and is situated in the southern section. Each of the two villages has a population figure of 3000.

Dhaisha camp lies 3 kilometres south of Bethlehem. It has a population of 5000 refugees. Tul-Karem camp is in the north of Nablus and, like Dhaisha camp, it is the subject of many curfews. The inhabitants of the two camps, originally, were a mix of urban and rural town-dwellers in pre-1948 Palestine, but belonged to the lower economic strata of the Palestinian society.

Each of the six urban centres was divided into four geographical areas extending from the town centre into East, West, North and South, for sample selection.

This method of selection was stipulated by poor town planning, particularly in metropolitan areas, which makes identifying streets and homes of interviewees an exhausting experience.

An alternative method, such as formulating a list of addresses from a local municipal authority, required an official approval of the military governor. Approval of this sort for similar studies in previous times was either delayed indefinitely or given but at a price. This time consuming-type exercise was thought to be a failure and was subsequently ignored.

The method of selection that was adopted was to select the respondents from every alternate house.

The survey itself was carried out and completed between September–December 1982. Ten Bir-Zeit university students from the Sociology Department constituted the basis of the interviewing team. They were briefed on the most conceivable administrative and circumstantial difficulties which they could encounter during the field survey. The interviewers were equally divided between males and females. As in other places in the Middle East, it is much easier on the West Bank for a female, for example, to communicate with wives and to gain entry into their homes.

This is especially true in conservative families where a married woman finds it inappropriate to allow a male stranger into the house if the husband is away. Indeed, it is not unusual that potential visits of this kind could arouse suspicions and have adverse effects to the reputation of the housewife. Further, a wife may feel less embarrassed in the presence of a female interviewer and may be less reserved about answering questions related to private thoughts and feelings.

The following were the criteria which each of the respondents was required to meet in order to qualify for the survey:

a) For female interviewees, any married women who was 18 years and above, was qualified to represent the household. This would exclude any other wife who may be living in the same house. Divorcees and widows were also excluded from the selection process.

b) For male interviewees, any married man who was 18 years and above, was qualified to represent the household. This also excluded grandfathers and children who may be residing in the same household. Divorcees and widowers were likewise excluded from the selection process.

The rationale behind not selecting both spouses from the same household ensured a wide-ranging sample and diverse information as responses dealt specifically with role relationships between spouses.

The response rate was over 90% of which 113 required a second visitation since the occupants were away or ill.[4] Another 49 refused to be interviewed because they suspected motives behind the survey. In all 1000 interviews were secured but 75 of these were confiscated from one interviewer by the military, thus reducing the sample to 925. (The student was put into custody for two nights as a result.) Data on the size distribution and other demographic characteristics of the sample will be outlined in a discussion which follows at a later chapter.

[4] In his book, *Survey Methods in Social Investigation*, 1958, Moser contends that a response rate less than 20% is considered valid in the 'average' survey; see also Lininger, C. G. *op. cit.* 1975 (p.192).

As age was the primary independent variable respondents were ultimately grouped into:

a) 'young married' adults, under 33 years,
b) 'middle-aged' between 34–53,
c) 'elderly age' at 54 years and over.

Across the three age groups, certain consistencies of similarity and regularities of difference were expected. The aim of this study is to explain and exemplify results according to select indications.

C: In The Field

The majority of interviews were made on first contact, without prior knowledge or arrangement, although appointments were necessary with a few people holding professional careers. All interviews were conducted in Arabic.

In the first moments of the interview the interviewer was instructed to introduce him/herself as a student at Bir-Zeit University. This was necessary to avoid suspicions of being mistaken for a government representative whose mission was to collect private information.

Surprisingly a minority of the Jerusalem sample presumed that the study was intended to promote the welfare of the community. Enquired one respondent: 'What can you do about them (apparently referring to his newly divorced neighbours). You must visit them, not us'.

Similar reactions often hindered the systematic administration of the survey which had been intended. However, these reactions allowed valuable insights into the socio-economic conditions and life-styles in general. It is recalled that on a number of occasions female respondents insisted on detailing their domestic problems, or problems with the health or ministerial authorities. The subjects of inflation and cost of living were favourites. Otherwise, the average length of each of the interviews was 35–40 minutes.

It was most expedient to visit homes in the mornings as the wives were likely to be there. Early hours of the morning proved sometimes useful in overcoming problems of privacy.

In larger families the situation invited problems galore, especially when the house was a small one. It was an inescapable case of family members being present or neighbours being called to provide a feeling of security in the absence of the household head. A case in point is related to questions on one's attitudes to marital problems which were viewed with intrigue in the presence of others; subjects of this sort are never talked about to strangers. Instructing others to keep quiet or to remain indifferent to the brief encounter turned into an aborted strategy. On these occasions interviews were interrupted by a barrage of curious questions, offers of coffee, drinks and sometimes meals.

Further, it was observed that the presence of the respondents' associates is an assured reminder that what they say should represent the opinion of the whole family. Despite lapses of interruptions, opinions of those present were accommodated artistically but never in writing.

After the identity of the researcher was established suspicions of instant recording of responses became neutralised and the survey drew such blessing as 'may Allah make you succeed and guard your dignity'.

A few of the verbal and gesticulative reactions that were displayed during some interviews might appear offensive, bizarre or idiosyncratic to the Western mode of thinking, but they are normal reactions in a Middle Eastern milieu. For example, in response to a question as to his marital status, a middle-age man remarked 'yes and no'. Said another 'where do you think these ratbags (apparently pointing to his children) came from?' Yet others left the researcher in suspense by replies such as 'write it as you wish', or, 'as you see' or simply 'well what do you think?'

Only a small minority considered the interviews an intellectual exercise. In one instance, remarked an old man in a challenging tone of voice, 'you just ask anything you want, and I give you enough information to start a whole new book'. In the course of the interviews, however, the role was often reversed so that the interviewer was regularly asked about his own personal opinion on a number of issues; a reaction perhaps based on an interest that every Palestinian seems to have in an explanation to social changes under the military occupation.

In all, it is generally conceded in most Arab societies that the subject of the family is a very sensitive and private matter. Difficulties in extracting accurate reliable information from subjects are immense. There are many cultural, structural and political factors behind it, especially during the past decade.

Israeli government representatives, then, have been collecting information on a regular basis regarding income tax, social welfare and social services within the Arab community in East Jerusalem.

On other occasions house searches have been taking place quite frequently on the pretext of national security. This often resulted in taking individuals into custody, confiscation of their identity cards, causing physical harm to suspected individuals and their property or simply placing them under house arrest.[5]

To illustrate this, Article 24 of the Defence (Emergency) Regulations,[6] which applied only to Palestinians living in Israel, states that 'a person who maintains contact with a foreign agent without having a reasonable explanation for doing so shall be deemed to have delivered secret information without being authorised to do so'. Also, 'any person who is in the company of a foreign agent or has in his possession the name or address of a foreign agent without having a reasonable explanation for his so doing or for such fact shall be treated as a person who maintains contact with a 'foreign agent'. A foreign agent is one who invites reasonable cause to suspect that he has engaged in the collection of secret information or any other activities calculated to impair the security of Israel. Usually, 'reasonable explanation' is one which the Israeli authorities considered 'reasonable'.

In conclusion, the process of giving personal information about oneself or family makes one feel vulnerable to unexpected results. Naturally, the attitude of Palestinians to surveys, by and large, has been one of suspicion towards the intention of those who collected data.

The second observation concerns the dominance of religious beliefs and values and the general subjection of the females opinions to the household head, which serve as indicators to conservatism.

Topics related to sexual relations and political affiliations were considered taboo, and subsequently prompted questions in the pilot study to be modified or omitted. This also applied to the subject of Islam. Not only is it considered the path to a better way of life, but it determined one's worldly way of life, one's viewpoints and social behaviour.

Socio-political questions of a sensitive nature are also con-

[5] Reports cited regularly in the *Jerusalem Post, Newsweek*, etc.

[6] Report of the State Controller in the Organisation for Security for the financial year 1957/58, No. 9, Feb. 15th 1959 (p.56) (in Hebrew).

sidered. Very rarely does the interviewer draw information which is not affected by the interviewee's suspicion that he/she is working in favour of one side or the other.

It was also observed that where age gives status in the whole Orient young interviewers rarely inspired confidence, regardless of their educational background.

Other difficulties are related to unwillingness or inability of the respondents to make a fine distinction of what 'controlling youngsters' meant. A sizeable percentage of the sample disregarded the role of elder male children, for instance in controlling younger brothers and sisters. This is contrary to what the Arab cultural norms usually dictate.

These difficulties naturally placed many limitations in securing sufficient information for a detailed analysis on some areas of change. They should, however, serve future researchers with some insight as to how these problems might be resolved.

In summary, the following observations should be made. Generally most of the rapport was rated as either good or reasonable. There were, of course, exceptions with respondents who were either very sensitive and inhibited or quite genuine and spontaneous.

Further, not all of the interviews were carried out inside the houses of the respondents. The responses of the interviewees were recorded verbatim and visible to them. At the end of each session, further comments and impressions were written down away from the respondents' presence.

By administering a sizeable number of questionnaires, formality was noticeably dissipated and more information was eventually obtained.

It should also be stated that there were moments of 'paranoia' that caused unfriendly suspicions or unusual reserve. In fact, some interviewees agreed to be interviewed only after skimming through the questionnaire.

D: Computations and Data Analysis

All of the data gathered in the survey underwent different processes of computer analysis. Frequency distribution of interval scale-values was the procedure adopted to handle the large quantities of data in the simplest manner. This technique was useful in that it enabled us to examine the characteristics of both dependent and independent variables.

The first part of the process, which is simply aimed at detecting and eliminating errors to the maximum, is identified as editing.[7] Dull as it may seem, this process plays an important role in coming up with accurate and hopefully complete answers. Even the most skilful interviewer is bound to omit some answers or even mark them in the wrong place. Mistakes are certain to occur with the presence of a human element, particularly in large-scale surveys.

The survey was completed by the interviewers under the supervision of the researcher. During the second stage, they checked that every question met with a response. After questions that contained no response were given a 'non-response' value. In a number of instances which involved cross-tabulation the above response was aggregated with 'not applicable'. With regard to open-ended questions the diverse responses which were obtained were given a numerical value, and were aggregated whenever necessary in a special 'scoring book'. In so doing the researcher was able to 'mop-up', as it were, all the dirty information.

Concrete assistance was further sought from a colleague at Bethlehem University Computer Centre; a physicist who assisted by providing insight on transferring the value number of every response to a 'coding system sheet' for the purpose of typing it into the computer. The numbers were then verified, counted and sorted out for each questionnaire.

With regard to some open-ended answers, the coding procedure was a little disheartening, due to a few responses being too odd or too deviant from the norm. A case in point, in response to 'what is the most pleasing aspect in your marital life?' The answer was 'ready meals, washed shirts and ironed trousers'. It is fortunate that the 'aggregate' categories were flexible enough to accommodate diverse responses.

Still, a few other responses were *recorded* in the same fashion for the purpose of effective cross-tabulation. However, the original values were retained in order to provide guide-lines for detailed analysis. At a final stage, all of the variables, the corresponding questions and the frequency of responses were recorded in a special coding book, designed for that purpose.

[7] Moser, C. G. and Kalton, G. *Survey Methods in Social Investigation*, London, 1971 (p.411).

When the data was clear, a number of programmes were designed in order to obtain frequencies and cross-tabulations. The latter required the use of the computer system (SPSS) which was designed to provide the user with comprehensive procedures of data analysis and manipulation without requiring any prior experience. This task was completed at the computer centre at Boga-Zichi University in Istanbul and lasted a period of four months.

Chapter 4

Demographic Characteristics

To this date there is no precise scientifically compiled information covering demographic aspects of West Bank Palestinians. Apart from few articles and reports which relate mainly to economic status nothing of value has come to light. Much of the data that is found in *Statistical Quarterlies* on administered territories seem to conflict with data reported by United Nations agencies. As such, we were obliged to be reserved about whatever available data existed. It should be noted, however, because of a homogeneity in their background, data collected on refugee camps would be expected to be the same irrespective of geographical areas.

Population Distribution and Characteristics

The West Bank, in addition to Gaza Strip, are the only British-mandated Palestinian areas which remained under Arab sovereignty between 1948 until the Israeli occupation in 1967.

Since its integration to the Hashmeite Kingdom of Jordan in 1948, the West Bank population was composed of two categories; pre-1948 refugees who fled as a result of the then Arab–Israeli War from their original villages and cities and the indigenous residents of the West Bank.

Palestinian camps were set up on small areas of uncultivated sites. When they were originally set up in 1950 they were primitive to the extreme, until gradually tents gave way to shacks, and later on houses replaced traces of previous dwellings. The largest of these houses consists of two bedrooms. During the sixties the

United Nations Relief and Works Agency (UNRWA) introduced basic amenities such as schools, water distribution systems and electricity. Nevertheless, the severely crowded conditions, basic gas heating and cooking devices do not escape the eye. For example, in the two sampled refugee camps, less than 0.3% were known to have a telephone.

The West Bank population was estimated at 981,000 Palestinians immediately after 1967, and they lived in an area totalling 5500 square km.[1] The area consists of the central part of what was called 'Palestine' during the British mandate. Most of its (Arab) urban settlements fall between its three main cities; Hebron, in the South, Jerusalem in the centre and Nablus in the North.[2]

In 1980, the total West Bank population was distributed into 64.5% rural dwellers, 25.5% urban settlers, and 10% (or 82,299) residing in refugee camps.[3] This pattern of distribution is close to that in East Jordan. The urbanised population there, *i.e.* those numbering 20,000 or more in a given area of settlement, is 44%. The rate of urbanisation has in recent years been increasing at a much faster rate than the world as a whole.[4]

1 Royal Scientific Society, *The significance of some West Bank resources to Israel* (Amman, 1974) (p.4); Efrat, E. 'Settlement pattern and economic changes of the Gaza Strip, 1947–1977' *The Middle East Journal*, 1977 (p.349); Jordan Department of Statistics *Main Findings of Advanced Tabulations; Housing and Population Census of 1979*. Amman 1981 (p.1).

2 Excluded from the focus of our study are the Jewish communities on the West Bank as well as those residing in (Arab) East Jerusalem. (They numbered 91,617 in April 1979 according to the R.S.S., *op. cit.* (p.5).)

3 UNRWA Report *Palestine Refugees in the Near East, Palestinian Refugees in the West Bank*, January 1980.

4 Ibrahim, S. 'Urbanisation in the Arab World' *Population Bulletin of the UN*. ECWA No. 7, July 1974 (pp.74–102). With regards to mass communication Jordan was rated as average of the developing countries; see Sigelman, L. 'Lerner's model of modernisation: a re-analysis' *Journal of Developing Areas*, 1974 (pp.525–536).

Table I. *Area Distribution of Sample (controlling for sex)*

Area	*Male*	*Female (Frequency)*	*Total*
1. Hebron	100	100	200
2. East Jerusalem	97	100	197
3. Jiffna	70	64	134
4. Khader	75	71	146
5. Dhaisha (camp)	53	51	104
6. Tul-Karem (camp)	57	87	144
Total	452	473	925

Table II. *Area Distribution of Sample (controlling for age)*

Area	*'Young' Low–33 Years (Frequency)*	*'Middle-aged' 34–53 Years*	*'Old' 54–Over*	*Total*
1. Hebron	119	71	10	200
2. East Jersualem	44	120	33	197
3. Jiffna	38	62	34	134
4. Khader	73	58	15	146
5. Dhaisha	61	35	8	104
6. Tul-Karem	48	80	16	144
Total	383	426	116	925

Table III. *Place of Birth (of sample)*

Area	*Frequency*	*Percentage*
1. Hebron	191	20.6
2. East Jerusalem	166	19.9
3. Jiffna	78	8.4
4. Khader	131	14.2
5. Dhaisha	16	1.7
6. Tul-Karem	36	3.9
7. Other Areas (West Bank)	160	17.3
8. East Jordan	20	2.2
9. Arab/Western World	22	2.4
10. Pre-1948 Palestine	105	11.3

B: Labour Force and Economic Structure

Since the 1948 Palestinian crises and after being expelled from the land of their ancestors, the new generation moved away from agriculture into technical and skilled professions in the urban areas which they migrated to.

By 1967, most of the refugee labour force from the camps started working in nearby towns, and the diversity of the work they undertook was on par with city residents.[5]

After 1967 most of the labour force dissolved into the Israeli economic system as unskilled labour in various industries and construction.

Table IV. *Distribution of West Bank and Gaza Palestinian Labour Force inside Israel, 1981*

West Bank Palestinians			*Gaza Palestinians*		
West Bank	*Israel*	*Total*	*Gaza*	*Israel*	*Total*
93.5	39.9	133.4	46.6	35.9	82.5

Source *Yearly Statistical Bulletin for West Bank and Gaza* 1982 (In Arabic) (No. 3)
Rural Studies Centre – An-Najah University Nablus (Table No.20,I).

Table V. *Occupational Distribution of West Bank Palestinians Working Inside Israel Between 1970 and 1977*

Year	*Agriculture*	*Industry*	*Construction*	*Percentage ratio of total Palestinian Labour Force*
1970	2600	1900	8000	12.8
1977	4500	8000	15,700	27.9

Source Abu-Lughad, J. *Demography of the Palestinians* (translated from Arabic) Jerusalem, Arab Studies Society, 1982 (p.117).

[5] Shamir, S. 'West Bank refugees between camps and society' in Migdal, J. (*ed.*) *Palestinian Society and Politics*, New Jersey, Princetown University Press, 1980 (p.147).

The overall depressed economic situation on the West Bank has certainly been a major factor in raising the percentage of Palestinians working in Israel. It must be remembered, however, that permanent employment is something rare for these workers as the majority are employed on a daily basis. The figure regarding those who work in Israel in Table VI, below, is rather small in proportion to the national figure. If, however, the housewives, who constitute 42% or 387, are excluded from the West Bank category then the percentage of those working in Israel becomes 75%. In addition, a sizeable percentage of workers consider working on Israeli settlements on the West Bank not the same as working in Israel.

Table VI. *Place of Work (of sample)*

Place of Work	*Frequency*	*Percentage*
1. West Bank	853*	92
2. Israel	40	4
3. Arab/Western countries	27	3
4. Missing values	5	1
	925	100

*Included in these categories a total of 387 housewives, or 42%.

Despite the obvious increase in the magnitude of labour force amongst West Bankers between 1970–1979 the ratio of female workers was proportionally stable, estimated at 31,000 or 8.6% of the total labour force. Yet, during the same stretch of time the number of females above the age of 14 increased by 75,000.[6]

The two most striking features between the two aforementioned tables are the housewife/husband and the professional categories. Constituting 8.5% of the total female sample, professional women come close in ratio to professional men, who constitute 11.3% of the male sample.

Though the male–female ratio is very close in the professional category, the figure of the housewives come to a high 81.8%. In

[6] Abu Kishek, B. *Report on the industrial and economic trends in the West Bank and Gaza Strip prepared for the economic commission for Western Asia B.Z.U. Research Centre*, Aug. 1981.

Table VII. *Occupational Distribution of Females (of sample)*

Occupation	*Frequency*	*Percentage*
1. Housewife	387	81.8
2. Professional	40	8.5
3. Clerical/skilled	13	2.7
4. Semi-skilled	1	0.2
5. Unskilled	10	2.1
6. Student	2	0.4
7. Unemployed	8	1.7
8. No answer	12	2.5
	473	100

Table VIII. *Occupational Distribution of Males (of sample)*

Occupations	*Frequency*	*Percentage*
1. House Husband	–	–
2. Professional	51	11.3
3. Clerical/skilled	94	20.8
4. Semi-skilled (trade/agricultural)	64	18.2
5. Unskilled (industrial/transport/construction)	235	49.8
6. Student	1	0.2
7. Unemployed	16	3.5
8. No answer	1	0.2
	452	100

this regard Basson notes about their East Jordanian counterparts, that they (women) are still regarded with suspicion if they are employed in the public sphere.[7] She writes:

> "she has two full time jobs: one as a wage earner and one as a home maker. Her entry into the public sphere is not matched by a corresponding entry of her husband into the private sphere of housekeeping and childcare. Her home making activities are conducted in a manner of keeping up with day-to-day demands."[8]

[7] Basson, P. *op. cit.* (p.66).

[8] *ibid*. p.66.

Lest the above observation leads us into a developed analysis of the division of labour between the sexes, a later chapter is devoted to examining this very subject. It is sufficient to draw the reader's attention to the fact that traditionally Palestinian women have worked in the field as well as at home.[9] Though they have been known to sell poultry and agricultural produce by the roadside and in public areas and markets in the West Bank main towns, they would still identify their 'profession' as housewife. The marginal income they bring home, in comparison to their spouses, and the longer hours of the day which they spend at home have contributed to this identification.

No shame is actually attached to village and a few refugee camp women in selling items in public places, though purchasing goods from stores is an activity that usually belongs to the household male head, who usually does this in the company of his younger male children.

With regards to town females, they are equally limited in their activities, if they engaged themselves in a purchasing activity, it is normally done in the company of female relations.[10]

Table IX. *Distribution of Occupations Across Three Generations*

Occupation	*'Young'* < *33 years*		*'Middle-aged'* *34–53 years*		*'Old'* *54 + years*	
1. Housewife	166	43.3%	185	43.4%	36	31.0%
2. Professional	38	9.9%	45	10.6%	8	6.9%
3. Clerical/skilled	40	10.5%	58	13.6%	9	7.8%
4. Semi-skilled	34	8.9%	29	6.8%	2	1.7%
5. Unskilled	93	24.3%	98	23.0%	44	37.9%
6. Student	3	0.8%	–	–	–	–
7. Unemployed	5	1.3%	7	1.6%	12	10.3%
8. No answer	4	1.0%	4	0.9%	5	4.3%
Total	383	100%	426	100%	116	100%

9 Fuller, A. *Buarij: Portrait of a Lebanese Muslim Village*, Harvard University Press, 1961 (p.73); Granquist, H. *Marriage Conditions in a Palestinian Family*, 1931 (p.20); Williams, H. & J. 'The extended family as a vehicle of cultural change', *Human Organization*, Vol. 24, 1965, p.63.

10 Patai, R. *Golden River to Golden Road: Society, Culture and Change in the Middle East*, 1969 (pp.131–3).

Table X. *Distribution of Occupations Across Areas*

Occupation	*Cities* Jerusalem/Hebron		*Villages* Jiffna/Khader		*Camps* Dhaisha/Tul-Karem	
1. Housewife	157	39.5%	121	43.0%	109	43.0%
2. Professional	57	9.2%	17	6.0%	17	7.5%
3. Clerical/skilled	63	15.5%	29	10.5%	15	7.0%
4. Semi-skilled	6	3.0%	31	11.0%	22	11.0%
5. Unskilled	94	23.5%	71	25.0%	70	28.0%
6. Student	3	1.5%	–	–	–	–
7. Unemployed	10	2.5%	10	3.5%	4	2.8%
8. No answer	1	0.5%	1	0.7%	11	7.6%
Total	397	100%	280	100%	248	100%

The results in Table IX suggest marked differences between the three generations in the 'housewife' and 'unemployed' categories. The unskilled 'young' and 'middle-aged' sub-samples total 24.3% and 23% respectively; whereas, the unskilled 'old' sub-sample are close to 37.9%. The latter group has also a relatively high figure of unemployed individuals, reaching 10.3%, as opposed to a respective 1.3% and 1.6% in the young and middle-aged categories.

With the exception of the 'clerical/skilled' category in the subsequent Table X almost all of the (occupational) categories are equally distributed amongst the three generation sub-samples.

These results have their roots in the post-war altered state of the economy that did not favour the younger generation into select occupational categories. Reasons and detailed analysis of this point have already been explored.

Conclusions

Obstacles to economic growth on the West Bank after 1967 are widely reported; and its effect on a Palestinian family is quite visible. For example, Mr. Benvenisti, former Deputy Mayor of Jerusalem, who heads a Jerusalem-based research institute stated that 'Israel has approved 36.6% of the agricultural projects and 23% of the industrial expenditures proposed by the United States, local Palestinians and voluntary agencies'.[11] Other contributory factors include confiscation of agricultural land, which constitutes a sizeable part of the 55% appropriated West Bank land, lack of credit facilities, the absence of local 'after hours' transportation system and so forth.

The light regulations imposed on the movements of Palestinian workers assisted in their non-separation from the extended family. Likewise, there were restrictions of working in Arab countries including East Jordan, with no guarantees of re-entry to the West Bank.

The immeasurable barriers placed on West Bankers obtaining construction permits by the military authorities, coupled with the crippling effects of the high inflation of prices in Israel, caused an astronomical rise in house rents.

The effects of wage-labour opportunities contributed towards narrowing the social status changes, which was instigated by variations of family ownership of land as well as the marginalisation of agricultural land.[12]

Prior to these changes, particularly during the Jordanian regime, the extended family practiced a certain trade or skill on which depended the lives of its members. Such binding dependency often led the family members to adopt common ideology which had a strong influence on their unification and on strengthening their kinship ties.

C: Educational Characteristics

With respect to the general educational situation on the West Bank, there wasn't a single study or a general census that was undertaken since 1967 to show variations in the estimates relating to school enrolment or levels of literacy. Taken as a whole group, the ratio of Palestinians who have completed tertiary education is the highest amongst Arab national groups with a total of 7.6%.[13] The figures obtained in the survey (Table XI) is well within reach.

[11] Quoted by the *Jordan Times*, April 12th–13th 1984 from the *Jerusalem Post*.

[12] Tamari, S. 'Building other people's homes' *J.P.S.* Vol. XI, No. 1, Autumn 1981 (p.80).

[13] See Zureik, E. *et. al., op. cit.*, 1980.

Table XI. *Level of Education*

	Frequency	*Percentage*	
1. No Education	133	14	
2. Primary education (part or all)	269	29	
3. Secondary: (form 1–3)	191	21	43
4. Secondary: (form 4–6)	199	22	
5. Tertiary : (part or all)	64	7	
6. Diploma of Higher Education (above secondary – college or institute)	69	7	

The figures in Tables XII and XIII clearly attest to changes towards an increase in the level of education amongst the 'young' generation for both males and females. It is possible, however, that because age distribution is skewed away from youngsters (15 years and younger) the demand on university education is on the decrease.[14]

Table XII. *Level of Education (male sub-sample)*

Occupation	*'Young' to 33 years*		*'Middle-aged' 34–53 years*		*'Old' 54 + years*	
1. No Education	1	0.5%	9	4.6%	18	23.7%
2. Primary: (part or all)	31	17.1%	69	35.4%	33	43.4%
3. Secondary: (part or all)	110	60.8%	79	40.5%	17	22.4%
4. Tertiary: (part or all)	17	9.4%	25	12.8%	6	7.9%
5. Diploma of Higher Education (above secondary – college or institute)	22	12.2%	13	6.7%	2	2.6%
	181		195		76	

Chi-square = 97.51960 with 10 degrees of freedom
Cramer's V = 0.32844; significance = 0001%

14 It is estimated that Palestinians who are younger than 15 years constitute 50% of the total population; see Hagopian, E. and Zahlan, A. 'Arab population in Palestine; demographic study of Palestinians' *JPS*, Summer 1974 (pp.32–73).

The educational standards of the female sub-sample, with regards to their male counterparts, are marginally at variance. As in the male sub-sample, the high percentage of illiteracy amongst older women (especially in refugee camps) is unquestionably due to the lack of educational facilities, which many young Palestinians experienced after the 1949 crisis. As regards the potential decline in the quality or standard of education for any age category it can be attributed to two main reasons; firstly, the dwindling funds and contributions of UNRWA; and secondly, the increasing control of teaching material and curriculum by the Israeli authorities.[15]

Table XIII. *Level of Education (female sub-sample)*

	'Young' to 33 years		*'Middle-aged' 34–53 years*		*'Old' 54 + years*	
1. No Education	13	6.5%	73	31.7%	19	47.5%
2. Primary (part or all)	45	22.4%	76	33.0%	14	35.0%
3. Secondary (part or all)	113	56.3%	64	27.8%	6	15.0%
4. Tertiary education (part or all)	11	5.5%	5	2.2%	–	–
5. Diploma of Higher Education (above secondary – college or institute)	19	9.5%	12	5.2%	1	2.5%
	201	100%	230	100%	40	100%

Chi square = 85.64783 with 10 degrees of freedom
Cramer's V = 0.30153; significance = 0.0001%

The two preceding tables clearly show that age differences in education are greater in the preceding generations. Both males and females of 'young' generation are better educated than older ones. Women, in particular, have made noticeable progress in the tertiary category even though their ratio is almost half of that of

[15] In R. Patai's book, *The Hashemite Kingdom of Jordan*. Human Relations Area File (1958) he states that as a general observation, Palestinian refugees have been better educated and more urbane than East Jordanians.

their sexual counterparts. Indeed, the parents' traditional attitude that females are more exposed when they are outside their role centre at home is on the wane.

Modesty code could not but be gradually modified in order to accommodate to the desire of educated daughters. Likewise, highly educated and skilled individuals have emerged under the rule of occupation, including social workers, teachers, skilled technicians and research assistants, as the feeling of national consciousness has steadily intensified.

As a general remark, however, the women's impressive strides in educational achievements, did not result always in gainful employment (Table VII, Chapter 4). The lag between their employment and education is not surprising in the context of traditional values on which the culture stands. This lag, however, should not be viewed as a reliable indicator of women's lack of desire or inability to work.

A final cursory glance at figures obtained for the whole sample as distributed over the six surveyed areas (Table XIV) shows that camp refugees reflect the highest proportion of illiteracy (Dhaisha 21.2%, Tul-Karem 34.0%) followed by villagers (Jiffna 9.0%, Khader 21.2%) and it diminished remarkably with city dwellers (Hebron 4.5%, Jerusalem 5.1%). At the other end of the scale, city dwellers reflect the highest level of tertiary education, with Jerusalem constituting 13.0% and Hebron 11.2% of their total samples. The ratio of tertiary educated village inhabitants constitutes 3.7% of the Jiffna sample and 3.4% for Khader. The ratio of tertiary educated people from Dhaisha refugee camp stands at 4.8% and from Tul-Karem camp at 7%.

D: Age at Marriage

For women, early age at marriage has been a culturally rooted norm within the Palestinian society. The parents' fear for their daughters' possible involvement in sexual, emotional relationships has, for a long time, been a strong preventive social force.

The polarised sexual attitudes between sexually-restricted females and relatively free-moving males seem to be the major factor behind females marrying at a younger age. In most middle Eastern cultures, the rigid code of male honour (*ird*) has virtually predetermined both the destiny and behaviour of women. This

Table XIV. *Level of Education (controlling for area distribution)*

	Hebron		*Jerusalem*		*Jiffna*		*Kḥader*		*Dhaisha*		*Tul-Karem*	
1. No Education	9	4.5%	10	5.1%	12	9.0%	31	21.2%	22	21.2%	49	34.0%
2. Primary (part or all)	44	22.0%	64	32.5%	38	28.4%	51	34.9%	15	14.4%	57	39.6%
3. Secondary (part or all)	96	48.0%	92	46.7%	71	53.0%	55	37.7%	46	44.2%	30	20.9%
4. Tertiary education (part or all)	26	13.0%	22	11.2%	5	3.7%	5	3.4%	5	4.8%	1	0.7%
5. Diploma of Higher Education (above secondary – college or institute)	25	12.5%	9	4.6%	8	6.0%	4	2.7%	16	15.4%	7	4.9%
	200		197		134		146		104		144	

thought will be expounded on further in the following chapter.

As independence increases with growing older, the development of alternatives to the traditional wife-and-mother role, is being perceived as an immediate threat to a wide section of the West Bank community. Being exposed to alternative life-styles will teach them new desires, new images and satisfactions which have never been dreamt of before. It would be reasonable to observe that the reason why the majority of the female sample married at the early age of 16–20 years (Table XVI) is because higher education is regarded as secondary to marriage. The latter preference, in addition to child-bearing, was cited as the most pleasing function in their (women's) marital life.[16]

It is commonly agreed that at the age of 20, the male is considered to be at a suitably marriageable age; for the female it is 18. Though individuals marrying at 15 years and less were noted in the sample, the male/female ratio is immensely disproportionate.

Tables XV and XVI show that the mean age at marriage for the Palestinian male sub-sample is 23.6 years, and the female average is 19.6. The youngest males of the sample married at the age of 14. Comparatively the number of females who indicated their age at marriage as between 12–15 years was 75 or 16.7% of the total female sub-sample.

The proportion of ages of Palestinian females at marriage is significantly lower than that of their Lebanese counterparts who immigrated to Australia since World War II (df = 3.31, P = 0.001).[17] Explanations for this phenomenon include the fact that the Lebanese males migrate initially on their own, with ambitions to work hard and establish themselves economically. At a later stage they are able to send for the rest of their families. While this trend holds true for most of married Lebanese, unmarried males fall into a similar pattern. As soon as they amass a reasonable amount of money, single males return to their home village and make it known that they are seeking a bride who is willing to return to Australia.

Setting a date for marriage usually indicates readiness on the part of the bridegroom to purchase furnishings for their intended residence. If, however, the groom did not accumulate a good lump

16 See Table V in the Appendix.

17 Ata, I. W. 'The Lebanese community in Melbourne', unpublished thesis, University of Melbourne, 1979 (p.160).

sum of money to secure the purchase, the wedding date would eventually be postponed.

Until 1967, Palestinian males displayed similar patterns though their countries of temporary emigration were the Gulf, and to a lesser extent, the United States. Since 1967, however, it became much harder for single male emigrés to go to the West Bank with ease (Table XVII). Instead, the wife-to-be would venture outside her home town to join her future husband wherever he happened to live outside the West Bank.

As regards the 'younger' generation on the West Bank, the marital age gap seems to have narrowed noticeably (Chart I). The altered political and economic reality since 1967 may have been the main factors behind it.

Table XV. *Age Frequency Distribution for Males at Marriage*

Class	*No. of males*
15 years	9
16–20	112
21–25	184
26–30	110
31–40	30
	Total 445
$\overline{X}$ = 23.66	

Table XVI. *Age Frequency Distribution for Females at Marriage*

Class	*No. of females*
12–15 years	75
16–20	214
21–25	116
26–30	30
31–35	14
	Total 449
$\overline{X}$ = 19.68	

Table XVII. *Place of Work (920 cases)*

Place of work	*Frequency*	*Percentage*
West Bank	853	92
Israel	40	5
Other (Arab and Euro-American Countries)	27	3
Missing value = 5	920	

E: Family Size

The main feature of the Palestinian family is a patriarchal extended unit. This has also brought with it a larger number of children than the family in an industrial society including that in Israel. Lerner reports that Palestinian Moslems during the fifties were estimated to have the highest birth rate in the world of 54 per 1000.[18]

The mean number of children per family in the survey sample was equated at 4.9. It is interesting to point out, however, that no significant differences were detected in the mean number of children between the urban and the rural sub-samples.

Table XIX. *Frequency Distribution of Number of Children Among Urban Families**

No. of children		*No. of families*
0 (no children)		32
1– 2		52
3– 4		162
5– 7		105
8–10		48
$\overline{X} = 4.2$	Total	397

*Jerusalem and Hebron sub-samples only

[18] Lerner, D. *op. cit.* (p.307).

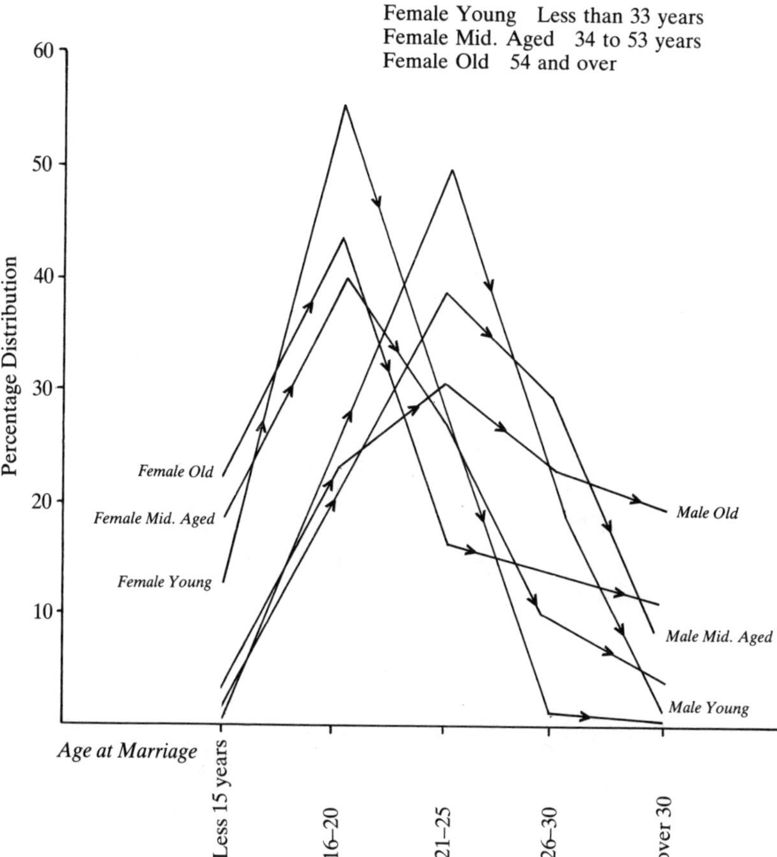

CHART I Age at Marriage (Young, Middle Age and Old; Male and Female Sul samples).

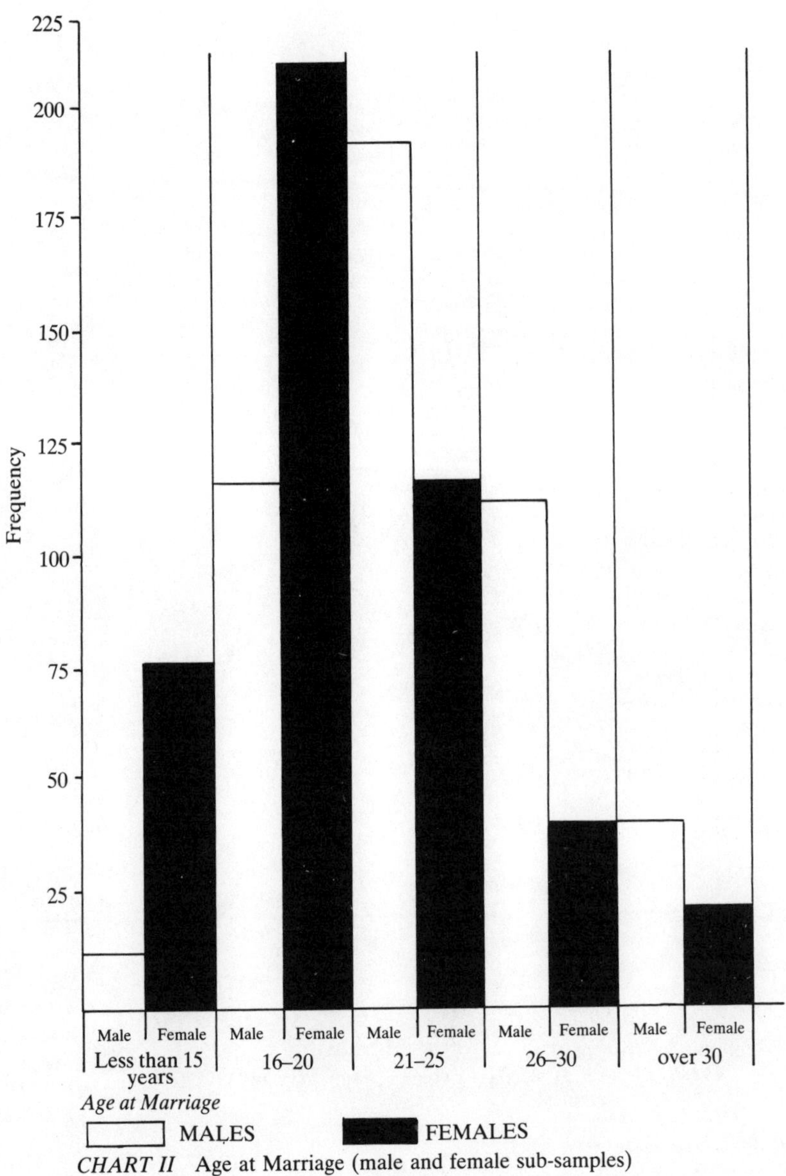

CHART II Age at Marriage (male and female sub-samples)

Table XX. *Frequency Distribution of Number of Children Among Rural Familes**

No. of children		*No. of families*
0 (no children)		24
1– 2		46
3– 4		181
5– 7		168
8–10		108
$\overline{X}$ = 41	Total	527

*Khader, Jiffna, Tul-Karem, and Dhaisha sub-samples.

F: Religious Affiliation

The combination of religion and nationality is a form of identification for the majority of Palestinians. The synthesised identity has, for centuries, influenced the sense of belonging, political life style and communal cohesion.

Historically, the fusion of the two elements (religion and nationality) was in response to the Turkish governments of each of the religious communities (*i.e.* millet)[19] as a distinct 'nationality'. Hunt[20] believes that the millet provided a system in which various groups could be ruled in most aspects of their lives by those with whom they shared common values.

Presumably different cultural traditions emerged across geographic boundaries because of the communities' isolation. The early churches simply evolved in different areas using languages

19 The 'millet' is a socio-political or communal organisation originally used by the Mamluks towards many groups who were in origin persecuted religious people seeking refuge in 'Greater Syria' and eventually gave rise to semi-independent religious communities. The organisation was later maintained by the Turkish government from the 15th to 19th centuries. The system was aimed at grouping new Turkish subjects (*i.e.* Christian and Jewish minorities) into separate communities.

20 Hunt, C. L. and Walker, L., *Ethnic Dynamics: Patterns of Intergroup Relations in Various Societies*, Homewood, Ill., Dorsey Press, 1974 (p.258).

and customs of particular places, their own bishops and even liturgy, though they maintained a viable relationship with the original apostolic churches in Jerusalem, Rome or Antioch.[21]

The West Bank has embraced various religious and ethnic groups in its fold: Greek Orthodox, Malkites (Greek Catholics), Protestants of all sects, Copts, Assyrians, Kurds, Armenians and Jews, only to name a few among the Christian affiliations. Moslems are also subjected to a similar formula of sectarian diversity. Against this it should be assumed that what is true of affiliates of one place will not always apply with respect to those of another. At the same time, throughout the centuries, inhabitants

Table XXI. *Religious Affiliation (of sample)*

	Frequency	*Percentage*
1. Moslems	714	77
2. Christians	209	23
3. M.V.	2	–

Table XXII. *Religious Affiliation (controlling for area distribution)*

Area	*Moslems*		*Christians*	
1. Hebron	200	100%	–	–
2. Jerusalem	116	59%	81	41%
3. Jiffna	11	8%	122	92%
4. Khader	143	98%	3	2%
5. Dhaisha	100	97%	3	3%
6. Tul-Karem	144	100%	–	–
Total	714	77%	209	23%

Chi-square = 559.69 with 5 degrees freedom; significance = 0.001
Cramer's V = 0.77871
Contingency coefficient = 0.61440
Lambda (asymmetric) = 0.16874 with *Area* dependent
= 0.53110 with *Religion* dependent
Lambda (symmetric) = 0.25000

[21] Congar, Y. *After Nine Hundred Years*, New York, 1957.

of different regions on the West Bank have undergone a remarkably uniform experience.

For this reason, attempts at introducing religious affiliation were put off for the future. Suffice it to observe that of those asked about their religion not one respondent abstained from identifying with the religion of his ancestry. The two missing values were the result of statistical errors.

Chapter 5

Honour, Pre-marital Encounters and Blood Relationships

Historical Perspective

For many centuries, the confinement of women and the segregation of sexes in Palestine, as in other parts of the Middle East, did not give women any chance to participate in the choices of their husbands. The opinions of her father and family, were decisive in the selection of a woman's marriage partner. Although the country's law may have required the consent of the bride as a prior condition for the drawing up of the marriage contract, in practice the (Moslem) girl did not attend the signing of the contract because her father testified on her behalf. Because she was not given sufficient freedom to mix with people of the opposite sex, the phrase 'what pleases my father pleases me' became an accepted dictum regarding the girl's choice of marriage partner.[1]

Marriage contracts were inevitably sealed by a bride-price paid to the parents of the wife-to-be, who were unwilling to part with their daughter without consideration. The bride-price also functioned as a guarantee that the young wife would be well treated in her new domain; otherwise it would become a source of support for the bride when divorced. While these practices were not so

1 Quote cited in Ata, I. 'Impact of Westernisation, and other forces on the Arab Moslem women in the Middle East', M.A. Thesis, University of Melbourne, 1975 (pp.112–113); see also Daghestani, K. *Famille Musulman Contemporaine en Syrie*. Paris, 1932 (p.13).

rigidly followed among Christians they still had some effect.

As tradition stipulated that marriage takes place at the hands of parents,[2] the man is expected to formally request the consent of the father before marriage proceeds. On certain occasions marriage was arranged at the time of the birth of the child.

However, the traditional culture provides an alternative to this requirement an equivalent to a Western elopement, with the couple facing severe family disapproval.[3] Ordinarily, the prospective groom, with the help of his friends, secretly removes his girl from her home. Later he returns to the village to attempt negotiations with the father through an intermediary. If these fail, the wedding is likely to proceed in any case, not in a church or a mosque, but outside the country and occasionally at the groom's house.[4] Such vestigial practices have been generally discarded by the well-to-do urbanised classes, but have been accepted on face value by others.

Relevant to the above observations are the concepts of honour, chastity and social organisation, which are clearly interconnected on the West Bank, and the Arab Middle East as a whole.

Honour of the men and the kinship is reinforced by the women following an ideal code of conduct and prescribed patterns of behaviour.[5] This indeed revolves around the chastity of women, which in turn is informally guarded by their immediate male relatives.

Based on the above association of notions are the following observations: a) a strong powerful authority in the hands of men who are considered as defenders of women's chastity; b) a clearly defined segregated male–female relationship; c) a well-structured status and hierarchy among members of the family.[6]

[2] Granqvist, H. *op. cit.*, 1935.

[3] Sweet, L. 'The women of Ain-Ed-Dayr' in *Anthropological Quarterly*, Vol. 40, 1947 (pp.176–183).

[4] *ibid.* (pp.179–180).

[5] Peristiany, J. G. *Honour and Shame, the Values of Mediterranean Society*. Chicago, University Press, 1966.

[6] Escribano, M. 'Honour, authority and social organisation in two West Bank Villages', paper delivered at State of the Art Symposium in Amman, Jordan, Feb. 25–28 1984 (p.1).

Relationship by Blood Prior to Marriage

The practice of maintaining family ties through 'blood marriage' has been common in most Middle Eastern cultures since the early days of civilization. Within the Palestinian culture there has been a consensus of feelings and opinions that marriage between relatives is definitely preferred to an exogamous counterpart.

In the 'Holy Land' marriage between blood relatives was recorded to be much esteemed as early as the second century; and 'the nearer the relationship the more highly it is esteemed'.[7] Not surprisingly, because blood relations between members of any large family are quite complex, the whole of the Middle East was termed a 'kinship culture'.

Chief amongst the criteria of appropriateness of a spouse aside from being of the same religion, class and, to a lesser extent, personal qualities, was family relations: first and second cousins usually. The ideal wife for a man is the daughter of his father's brother. If none is available, then he is encouraged to select a distant one.

Many reasons are provided for this preference, as cousin marriages are believed to bring with them fewer problems into the husband's household. They are said to make for smoother relations in the household, assure that the couple is well matched, maintain and strengthen existing kinship ties and cohesion among its members and preserve and arrange property within the kinship group.[8] Thus, as long as marriage takes place within the same lineage, women can inherit and transmit property.

This phenomenon raises an important anthropological question; since families of the bride and the bridegroom have a shared descent, how can marriage play a role which is not already considered superfluous? It is also presumed true that once marriage takes place for reasons of affection and love, the whole family structure would collapse.

Peters[9] illustrates that:

> "cross cousin marriages represent attempts to expand the total land holdings of an individual to extend a particular plot

[7] Wilson, C. *Peasant Life in the Holy Land*, London, 1806.

[8] Michaelson, E. and Goldschmidt, W. *op. cit.*

[9] Peters, E. 'Aspects of rank and status among Moslems in a Lebanese village' in Sweet, L. (*ed.*) *op. cit.* (p.111).

> or plots at a certain altitude. The significance of a particular marriage form lies not in the form itself but in the frame which it is set. The same form can make an estate or break it . . . (it) ensures that any marriage within the framework of which (an ancestor) is the apex retains property within the general state."

In addition to what was outlined earlier, preferential cousin marriages reflect concern for preserving premarital chastity in patrilineal families because of the patrilineal emphasis on producing legitimate male heirs.

Preference in cousin marriages is expressed in daily sayings such as: *Bint il amm Hammālit Il-Jafa, Amma il Gharībe Bidda Tadlil*, that is, the cousin (wife) can put up with austerity but a stranger needs looking after. And, *Ibn al-amm Abda*, or, the male cousin comes first. This has made it common practice for the man to address his wife in public places as *Ya Bint Ammi* (my father's brother's daughter).[10] This practice brought with it another phenomenon: symbiotic cousin marriages; that is, a family would consent to marrying off their son to his female cousin so long as her brother marries one of their daughters. Yet despite all this, one can still find brothers of one family married to sisters of another.

Granqvist, and other folklore and orientalist historians, give reasons additional to cultural ones for cousins' marriages. Economically speaking a man can obtain his cousin as a bride at a smaller price than he can obtain a stranger, they observe.

In her 1931 study of the Artas community on the West Bank, Granqvist found that 33.7% of the sample were in fact blood marriages, that 23.5% were married spouses from the same village but from different clans, and the remaining 42.8% were marriages between local males and women who were strangers.[11]

[10] A clear example of the male dominance is the fact that *Bint al Amm* (paternal female cousin) is considered a closer relative than *Bint al Khāl* (maternal female cousin) even though they are both first cousins. Sometimes the term *Ibn Al Amm* refers to a second cousin and other distant relationships so long as there is an understanding of a common origin, *i.e.*, forefathers. The term is also used in reference to any intimate relationship between spouses.

[11] Granqvist, H. *op. cit.* (pp.69–70).

Fifty years later, figures of blood marriages in the survey sample reflect almost similar patterns (Table I), thus indicating that cousin marriages are viewed as more advantageous and common than stranger marriages. Village and regional marriages were not introduced in a separate category. Likewise distant relationships, *e.g.* fourth cousins, were not considered as being blood relationships.

Table I. *Relationship by Blood (925 cases)*

Blood Relationship	*Frequency*	*Percentage*
1. Indicating 'yes'	390	42
2. Indicating 'no'	527	57
3. Missing value	8	1
	925	100

Yet, in spite of the relative stability and continuity of blood marriage tradition, some changes were noted from the traditional patterns between the 'young' and 'older' generations.

Table II. *Relationship by Blood (across 3 age groups)*

Blood Relationship	*Young (M1)*		*Middle-aged (M2)*		*Old (M3)*	
1. Indicating 'yes'	160	42%	177	41.5%	53	45.7%
2. Indicating 'no'	219	57%	245	57.5%	62	53.4%
	379		422		115	

$f = 10.13$ $f > F\ (0.95, 2.3) = 9.55$
Reject H_0 = M1 & M3 10.13>9.55
Kendall's Tau, $C = 0.01555$; Significance = 0.32
Gamma = 0.02642

Results obtained in the *t*-test determine that we reject the null hypothesis, but only between 'young' and 'old'; that is, there are no other significant differences in the means between either of the former two categories and the 'middle-age' group. In other words, there is a significant shift in the two sets of responses of having blood relationship, or otherwise, between the 'young' generation (younger than 33 years) and the 'older' one (older than 54 years).

Thus, 45.7% of the latter group do have blood relationship prior to marriage and 53.4% do not; whereas 41.1% of the younger group indicated that there is a relationship and 57.4% indicated otherwise.

The statistical decrease in endogamous marriage can be partly explained by the continuous migration of young males to more stable and economically and politically secure countries. It is generally true that a large number of males who go to study in western universities end up marrying there.[12]

Decreased endogamy can also be due to the growing outflow by young male workers to higher waged possibilities for unskilled workers in the Israeli market. In a way, male workers became freer in their movements and actions outside their village, which allows them more independence in making personal decisions.

One basic difference between Palestinian camps and villages and the cities is related to the basis and nature of their social organisation. Whilst cities are made up of a collection of individuals or families, camps (and villages) are highly cohesive structures 'whose families grouped around the Palestinian villages from which they originated and the extended family units are still the basis of social life'.[13] As such, the social consciousness of family regional ties and common origin became influencing factors which reinforced blood marriages in the same way that they used to happen before the 1948 exodus. Attitudes and social values which dominated village life, including respect of elders, sacrificing one's comfort for the sake of others and offering generosity, have all been transplanted and preserved.

Individual and communal attitudes have played a major role in preserving inter-communal marriages. Results obtained in Table III support the observation that with respect to blood marriages the proportion is relatively higher amongst villagers and camp refugees than in cities. The current figures are only slightly different from those obtained by Rosenfeld (p.46) in 1957, of a Palestinian village within the 1947 borders. His figures show that

[12] The number of Arab students, as a whole, who stayed in western countries after completing their higher studies are estimated at 60%; reference in the *Jordan Times* (19/12/1983) in *Controlled educational policy needed to regulate brain outflow* by Ibrahim Ata.

[13] Sirhan, B. *Palestinian Refugee Camp life in Lebanon* in S. Eddin Ibrahim, *op. cit.* (p.353).

almost 60% have been parental cousin marriages.[14] Noteworthy is that the majority of the Jerusalem sample (71.2%) are skewed away from blood marriages.

Shamir found that inter-marriage between refugee and non-refugee Palestinians was almost a non-event. The latter group, he observed, are quite reluctant to marry off their daughters to Palestinian refugees, since they are perceived as inferior and 'outside any binding code of traditions and customs'.[15]

Though this observation may correspond to reality to some degree, an appropriate test of significance is obviously needed here to validate such a conclusion.

Forces Behind Choice of Spouse

Preference of endogamous marriage is prevalent amongst and across various social classes: urban/rural families, and ethno-religious communities on the West Bank. This kind of social habit obviously limits one's choice and the availability of spouses.

A sizeable body of studies on marriage customs in the Arab World, including what was called Palestine in 1948, point out that little, if any, change in the search of spouses, pre-arranged marriages and blood relationships, have actually occurred.[16] Granqvist found, for example, little difference in the practices between Aratas and other Palestinian villages.[17]

Yet, despite the remarkable stability over time in such customs in the West Bank, changes have occurred across the three generations, as will be detailed later on.

Tradition in Palestine demanded explicitly that marriage take place at the decision of the parents.[18] As such, the man was not in a position to select his spouse, let alone given the chance to be alone

14 Rosenfeld, 'Analysis of marriage and marriage statistics in a Moslem–Christian Arab village' *International Archives of Ethnography*, Vol. 48, (1957) (pp.32–62).

15 Shamir, S. *West Bank Refugees Between Camps and Society* in Migdal, J. *ed. op. cit.* (pp.194–5).

16 Goode, W. *op. cit.*, 1963.

17 Granqvist, H. *op. cit.*

18 *ibid.*; Berelson, B. and Steiner, G. *Human Behavior: an Inventory of Scientific Finding*, New York, 1964 (p.397).

Table III. *Relationship by Blood (controlling for area)*

	Cities				*Villages*				*Camps*				
Blood Relationship	*Hebron*		*Jerusalem*		*Jiffna*		*Khader*		*Dhaisha*		*Tul-Karem*		*Total*
Indicating 'yes'	90	45%	55	29%	57	43%	74	51%	48	46%	66	46%	42.5%
Indicating 'no'	110	55%	136	71%	76	57%	71	49%	56	54%	78	59%	57.5%

Lambda (asymmetric) = 3.036 with *Area* (dependent) = 007 with *Blood relation* (dependent)

with her prior to his wedding date. In certain occasions, marriage was arranged at the time of the birth of the child.

In more rigid circumstances, a young man may not express his desire to marry a certain woman nor remind his parents of the timing of his wedding date, but had to submit to his parents' decisions. It is their prerogative to decide on the right times and the appropriate spouse. The actual search for the wife-to-be is undertaken by the parents or sisters, who would look for the suitable spouse who embodies qualities of honour, good reputation and ancestry and physical appearance.[19]

This observation is also applicable to females, in the sense that they have not been encouraged to level with their parents about their desires or the timing of their marriage.

Marriage was, therefore, a family affair, sanctioned by the society in full anticipation that a 'normal' person should ultimately become married. By making a choice about their son's spouse, the parents would have contributed towards reinforcing traditional values of authority and dependency.[20]

Table IV. *Person(s) who Selected Wives for Marriage*

	Responses			
Selectors	*Male*	*sub-sample*	*Female*	*sub-sample*
1. Husband	255	56.0%	168	36.0%
2. Wife herself	3	0.7%	33	7.0%
3. Husband's family	175	39.0%	153	32.6%
4. Wife's family	3	0.7%	83	17.7%
5. Relatives	7	1.5%	14	3.0%
6. Friends	6	1.3%	10	2.1%
7. No answer	3	0.7%	8	1.7%
	452		469	

The most apparent results which are not proportional between the male and the female sub-samples in Table IV are related to the first response. The fact that almost twice the ratio of husbands (56%) indicated that they selected their wives, as against that of the wives (36%) who indicated that their husbands selected them for marriage, reflects a diversity of attitudes. Overall the results

19 Goode, W. *op. cit.* (p.89).
20 Wittfogel, K. *Oriental Despotism*, New York, 1953 (Section on Oriental or Asiatic family).

echo the male's undisputed authority over (and pride in) the rest of his family. The fact that almost one third of the wives indicated that their husbands 'chose' them, reflect their acceptance of the practice of being passive in the whole affair. Interestingly however, as many as 33 wives (7.0%) indicated that they chose their husbands, as opposed to 3 husbands or (0.7%) who gave this kind of response.

Of the male sub-sample, 39% indicated that their family chose their wives, as opposed to 32.6% of the female sub-sample who gave the same response; *i.e.* their husband's family chose them. These sizeable figures illustrate clearly that the following custom is still alive: when the son reached a marriagable age, the father asks the female members of the family, who include the mother and sometimes the aunt and grandmother, to visit other 'appropriate' families in order to find an appropriate wife. It is noteworthy that the role of the mother often seems less crucial in selecting her son's wife than her daughter's husband.[21] Through females and relatives, the fathers meet and, if all goes well, give their stamp of approval to the final deal. Obviously, making a choice about their son's spouse has contributed to reinforcing the traditional value of parental authority and dependency.

There have been, amongst a few families in bigger towns, males alluding to their parents' preferences towards certain females. Often this would be short of taking a final decision by themselves, as the sons rarely go against the mother's objection if it is very strong. The mother may indirectly suggest alternatives to her son, but her suggestions are definitely important in his final choice. The only exception applies to his second spouse; that is, if his first one passed away, or divorce procedures are completed.[22]

Interracial and Interreligious Marriages

One of the most common forms of pressure used against free choice of one's spouse is religious endogamy. This means that the religious dogma towards marrying within the same sect is so strong that one is subject to excommunication from church if she or he was a Christian, as well as religious social grouping, to a lesser extent.

[21] Daghestani, K. (1952) *op. cit.* (p.127).
[22] *ibid.*

It is true that inter-sectarian marriages amongst Christians do take place, but the ceremony usually takes place in the church with which the bridegroom is affiliated.

Although statistics on inter-religious marriages are scarce, it is an event that is generally stigmatised by communities of the two great religions – Islam and Christianity. Not one household in the sample formed an inter-religious unit.

In addition to those who are apathetic about such form of marriages, the small percentage of Moslem respondents who indicated agreement, qualified their responses. In conformity with principles of the Koran, this group approved of marriages between Christian women and Moslem men, but not the opposite, on the grounds that children must adopt their father's religion. Likewise, a few Christians indicated similar feelings but less emphatically with regards to marriages between Christian men and Moslem women.

In the same pattern of preferences, marriages between West Bank females and non-Arab males is very rare indeed. Because this form of marriage is violently discouraged, the few cases who deviated from this norm have in fact resided in the countries of their bridegrooms.

The opposite kind of marriage, involving a Palestinian male and a Western female, is relatively much more common. Only a small percentage of this group continues to live on the West Bank, but for a different reason. Restrictions imposed by the Israeli government in granting residence permits to either Palestinians who were not included in the 1967 Israeli census for one reason or another, or foreign wives of Palestinians, have been so extreme that the latter group re-immigrated to the East Bank of Jordan and elsewhere.

The rationale given by those who expressed that inter-racial marriages are good, but only between Palestinian females and Western males was clear: Palestinian females are more likely to be faithful to their Western spouses than Western females to Palestinian husbands.

Though such a reaction does not necessarily represent attitudes of every member of the community, it does illustrate the restricting factors placed upon this kind of marriage. It is necessary to clarify that the word 'strangers' was used to denote the 'foreign' wife, who is an agent for the Westernisation of her children.

Marrying outside the community often leaves it with feelings of dissatisfaction, since the usual form it takes is Palestinian males marrying non-Palestinian women. In so doing, they deprive some Palestinian women of marriage for a lengthy period.

During the survey research one of the remarks which was expressed in respect of a 'Western' wife of a Palestinian male who re-immigrated to the West was:

> "Look at her kids, she comes and goes and nobody cares about them, even her husband does not dare to ask her where she goes. He knows she will divorce him and take his kids."

Dissatisfaction with Western family structures was also reflected in the following responses: 'but their divorce rate is high', 'they don't have family ties', 'they have sexual permissiveness at an early age', and, 'and who would then clean the house and cook the meals, wash the clothes and feed the kids? Do you really think the foreign wife would do all these things?'. The contrast in attitudes towards family life are probably summarised by Elkholy when he writes that those women 'outsiders' who marry Middle Eastern men:

> "find it hard to cross that rugged gulf to the extended family pattern of (her) husband. (She) finds herself aggravated and lost in an infinite number of relationships, each of which is traditionally prescribed and requires a set of specific mutual obligations".[23]

It would be fair to point out that in the past few years some families in a desperate tone remarked that it is much better for their children to marry foreigners and leave behind 'the miserable life under occupation', (interview 308).

A cursory glance at the results of Table V suggests a significant association in the relationship (Kendall test = 0.009) between the age of female sub-sample and the responses as to who selected them for marriage. As the sample becomes younger the tendency of future male spouses to have a final say in selecting their counterparts increases, whilst the tendency of the family of the male (and indeed the female) to select his wife (or her husband) for them decreases.

23 Elkholy, A. 'The Arab American Family' in C. H. Mindel *et al* (*eds.*) *Ethnic Families in America*, New York, 1976 (p.158).

Results obtained for the null hypothesis indicate that it must be rejected. That is, there is a significant shift in the means of the responses of firstly, the husbands, and secondly, the husbands' families, amongst the three generations.

Table V. *Female Sub-sample Responses of Persons Who Selected Them for Marriage*

Selector	*'Young' M1*	*'Middle-aged' M2*	*'Old' M3*
1. Husband	97	80	9
2. Husband's family	68	76	9
3. Wife's family	27	40	16

N = 339
f (0.95, 2, 3) = 0.955 $f>F$ Reject H_0 (M1, M2 and M3)
Kendall's Tau, C = 0.09262; Significance = 0.0097
Kendall's Tau, B = 0.9581; Significance = 0.0097
Gamma = 0.14747

Results obtained in Table VI show that at the 0.01 level of significance, there is an association in the relationship between age of male sub-sample and the responses. As to who selected their wives for marriage in the category of the 'young', for example, the ratio of those who indicated that they themselves chose their wives were twice as many (at 112) as those who indicated that their family had (61). It is not surprising to note that those who indi-

Table VI. *Male Sub-Sample Responses of Persons who Selected their Wives for Marriage*

Selectors	*'Young' M1*	*'Middle-aged' M2*	*'Old' M3*
1. Husbands 'themselves'	112	106	37
2. Husband's family	61	81	33
3. Wife's family	1	1	1

N = 430
f = 3.778; $f<F$ (0.95, 2, 3) = 9.55; 3.778<9.55
Accept H_0; M1 = M2 = M3
Kendall's Tau C = 0.07888; Significance = 0.0188
Gamma = 0.15672

cated their wife's family as the main selectors were much lower in frequency than those in the female sub-sample. The discrepancy in these attitudes is the result of the traditional Arab family, which is patriarchal, taking all major decisions and, where women have low status in the family, the women having little input in the family's decision making.

Though the level of association between the two variables is significant, the analysis of variance (*t*-test) indicates that the null hypothesis must be accepted. That is, there are no significant differences in the means of the responses amongst the three generations; *i.e.* there is no significant shift in the ratios of responses between the young, the middle-aged and the old.

Courtship and Pre-marital Speech

Free mixing between young Palestinian men and women especially in public places, is still largely foreign to the Palestinian West Bank culture. Yet, something close to it has been taking place on a limited scale amongst urban, educated and upper-income families who have Western ties. Co-educational classes in certain missionary administered schools, the four universities and in the very few religious oriented and scout-run clubs are common.

The Western-style romantic love and courtship is certainly imbued in Palestinian literature, but rarely between men and women who marry one another. The main theme of concern has been expressing the woman's attractive features, rather than creating a love story involving both her and the man's emotions; marriage has for a long time never been the consequence of love.[24]

If any emotions were revealed, they were those of the male, not the female. Although love sometimes grows between a husband and wife who had not been acquainted before marriage, they still go on living together without necessarily understanding each other. Subsequently, it is not strange to learn that women, for example, who did not have prior acquaintance with men accept whatever sentiments they felt towards their menfolk as love.

Ironically enough, married women on the West Bank enjoy greater freedom and mobility than unmarried girls. The fact that

[24] Berger, M. *The Arab World Today*. New York, Garden City, 1962 (p.24).

the odd male still seeks sexual relations with married women is a good evidence for such a hypothesis. The reason behind this might be the fact that the wrath of the husband is feared less than that of the father.

Repercussions and consequences of such a rigid code of behaviour are discussed in a later chapter on marital relationships.

Suspecting that the male sub-sample would, for obvious reasons, give biased responses to the following 'loaded' question; 'Had you ever spoken to your wife before marriage?' they were spared being put in the position to answer. Table VII shows that the female sub-sample was unproportionally divided between a sizeable 58% indicating that they never spoke to their husbands prior to marriage, and 40% indicating otherwise.

Table VII. *Responses to the Question: 'Had you ever spoken to your husband before marriage?' (female sub-sample)*

Responses to the Question	*Frequency*	*Percentage*
1. Indicating 'Yes'	190	40
2. Indicating 'No'	274	58
3. No answer	8	2
4. Missing value	1	–
Total =	473	100

Noteworthy is that the teachings of Islam go against the male and female communicating with one another unless the male declares his intention to marry her. The Koran implicitly states:

> "Tell the believers to turn away their eyes and to guarantee their salvation. Allah knows what is better for them."[25]

A cursory glance at the results in Table VIII suggests that the direction of the relationship between the two responses amongst the three generations is consistent with our hypothesis; that is, that there is an association in the relationship between the two variables (at 0.004):[26] firstly, age and secondly, premarital speech. It is apparent that the younger sub-sample displays a

[25] *Sura Al-Noor – 30.*
[26] Kendall's Tau *C*-test.

Table VIII. *Response to the Question: 'Had you ever spoken to your husband before marriage?' (female sub-sample; three generations)*

Responses	*Yes*		*No*		*Total*
'Young'	97	50%	97	50%	194
'Middle-aged'	81	35.5%	148	65.5%	229
'Old'	12	30%	28	70%	40

$f\,(0.95, 2, 3) = 9.55$; $f<F$ Accept H_0
Kendall's Tau C = 15851; Significance = 0.0004
Kendall's Tau B = 15050; Significance = 0.0004
Gamma = 0.28167

greater tendency to have verbal encounters with their wives-to-be, than the middle-aged or the older generations. The young sub-sample is equally divided between those who spoke with their wives prior to marriage (50%), and those who did not (50%). The middle-aged group includes a higher percentage of those who did not have pre-marital speech (65.5%) than the former group; whereas the 'oldest' group has the highest percentage (at 70%) of the three generations.

Though the level of association between the two variables is significant, the analysis of variance (*t*-test) indicates that the null hypothesis must be accepted ($f\,(0.95, 2, 3) = 9.55$, $f<F$); that is, there are no differences in the means of the responses among the three generations.

Despite the lack of significance in the ratio between the two responses of having or not having had pre-marital speech amongst the three generations, the direction of change, as indicated by the direction of the results, signifies some kind of shift in behaviour. Obviously, opportunities for developing encounters allowing for exchanges in intimacy and friendship have increased. No longer does the decision of elders in the choice of marriage partners for their youngsters determine, as in the past, whether or not wives have spoken with their husbands before marriage.

The 'younger' generation is starting gradually to meet one another privately and certainly talking with one another before marriage. The youngsters seem to be deviating from the norm whereby courtship takes place within the fiancé's house mostly in the presence of relatives. One must bear in mind, that courtship in the West Bank, and indeed in the rest of the Arab countries, is defined as the period between engagement and wedding – the time when the couple actually becomes acquainted.

Having analysed the current trends of courtship, a future study can be introduced to see whether or not spouses view meeting their future partners before marriage as unnecessary or not.

In retrospect, pre-arranged marriages including blood relationships and courtship trends undoubtedly have helped to reinforce cohesion amongst members of extended families. This has been true so long as Palestinian families have 'competed as factions, openly and violently in a struggle for security and political positions within the village, against other extended families (or *hamāyll*)'.[27] Pre-arranged marriages are another form of pledging allegiance to this social structure, which in turn fulfils one's social and welfare needs.

[27] Rosenfeld, J. *From Peasantry to Wage Labour and Residential Peasantry: the Transformation of an Arab Village* in Sweet, L. *op. cit.* (p.149).

Chapter 6

Decision Making and Family Authority Structure

Introduction

Making decisions and expressing one's opinion in formulating family decisions are signs of being in a position of power and authority. Conversely, being in a position devoid of power and authority would certainly signify absence in the participation of making decisions.

The aim of this section is to focus on the male/female power relations and the way which the authority structure varies with power distribution in the family at large, and across the three age groups.

A number of indicators were selected to suggest what, if any, changes in the direction of a greater freedom of choice, particularly for women and within different age groups, have taken place. The four major indicators were:

a) income of family
b) care of children
c) family entertainment
d) visitation of relatives

The four indicators were the target of two main questions: firstly, in your *current* marital life, who is (mainly) responsible for the following and, secondly, in an *ideal* situation, who, in your opinion, should be (mainly) responsible for the following.

The decisions were ranked in such a way that they allowed for a number of possible responses. The responses were aggravated into

Table I. *Male Sub-sample Responses to the Question: 'In your current marital life who is mainly responsible for the following?*

	Husband only		Wife only		Husband and wife		Mostly husband		Mostly wife		Equally husband and wife		Sons		Other sources		No answer	
Income	385	85%	3	1%	51	11%	8	2%	2	1%	0	0%	1	0%	1	0%	1	0%
Care of children	13	3%	281	62%	90	20%	3	1%	34	8%	2	1%	0	0%	0	0%	29	6%
Cleaning of house	6	1%	394	87%	15	3%	2	1%	33	8%	0	0%	0	0%	0	0%	1	0%
Discipline	15	3%	58	13%	298	66%	15	4%	33	8%	4	1%	0	0%	0	0%	28	6%
Entertainment	136	30%	36	8%	210	46%	30	7%	13	3%	12	3%	0	0%	0	0%	14	3%
Contact with relatives	90	20%	14	3%	258	57%	32	8%	12	3%	44	10%	0	0%	0	0%	2	1%

Table II. *Male Sub-sample Responses to the Question: 'In an ideal situation who, in your opinion should be mainly responsible for the following?'*

	Husband only		Wife only		Husband and wife		Mostly husband		Mostly wife		Equally husband and wife		Sons		Other sources		Society		No answer	
Income	331	73%	5	1%	99	22%	5	1%	1	0%	8	2%	0	0%	0	0%	2	1%	1	0%
Care of children	5	1%	251	56%	168	37%	0	0%	19	4%	9	2%	0	0%	0	0%	0	0%	0	0%
Cleaning of house	7	2%	360	80%	48	11%	4	1%	24	5%	3	1%	1	0%	0	0%	0	0%	0	0%
Discipline	29	6%	46	10%	347	77%	11	2%	11	2%	7	2%	0	0%	1	0%	0	0%	0	0%
Entertainment	129	29%	14	3%	265	59%	18	4%	6	1%	14	3%	0	0%	0	0%	2	1%	4	1%
Contact with relatives	98	22%	6	1%	292	65%	15	3%	2	1%	28	6%	0	0%	0	0%	3	1%	6	2%

Table III. *Female Sub-sample Responses to the Question: 'In your current marital life who is mainly responsible for the following?*

	Wife only only		*Husband*		*Husband and wife*		*Mostly wife*		*Mostly husband*		*Equally husband and wife*		*Sons*		*Other sources*		*No answer*	
Income	3	1%	385	85%	51	11%	2	1%	8	2%	0	0%	1	0%	1	0%	0	0%
Care of children	368	80%	7	2%	58	12%	24	5%	0	0%	2	1%	0	0%	0	0%	0	0%
Cleaning of house	419	89%	9	2%	16	3%	23	5%	1	0%	4	1%	0	0%	0	0%	0	0%
Discipline	175	38%	11	2%	197	43%	57	12%	9	2%	7	2%	1	0%	0	0%	0	0%
Entertainment	60	14%	67	15%	220	50%	23	5%	39	9%	26	6%	2	1%	0	0%	0	0%
Contact with relatives	42	9%	36	8%	263	57%	26	5%	24	5%	73	16%	1	0%	0	0%	0	0%

Table IV. *Female Sub-sample Responses to the Question: 'In an ideal situation who, in your opinion should be mainly responsible for the following?'*

	Wife only		*Husband only*		*Husband and wife*		*Mostly wife*		*Mostly husband*		*Equally husband and wife*		*Sons*		*Other sources*		*Society*		*No answer*	
Income	7	2%	211	45%	232	50%	2	1%	7	2%	6	2%	1	0%	0	0%	2	1%	0	0%
Care of children	249	53%	4	1%	174	37%	36	8%	1	0%	4	1%	0	0%	0	0%	0	0%	0	0%
Cleaning of house	341	72%	3	1%	80	17%	30	6%	1	0%	18	4%	0	0%	0	0%	0	0%	0	0%
Discipline	122	26%	16	4%	281	60%	10	2%	24	5%	14	3%	0	0%	0	0%	0	0%	0	0%
Entertainment	35	8%	66	5%	284	62%	10	2%	17	4%	36	8%	0	0%	0	0%	1	0%	0	0%
Contact with relatives	17	4%	30	6%	323	70%	13	3%	6	2%	76	16%	0	0%	0	0%	1	0%	0	0%

four different tables; two of which made up the male sub-sample and two the female sub-sample.

The results regarding Tables I and II clearly show that the weight of responses for both the male and the female sub-samples are uniform. That is, the majority of the two sub-samples indicated that the male (husband) is the provider for the family, whereas, the female (wife) was the housekeeper (cleaner) whose role was care of the children. Thus 85% of the male sub-sample and 85.4% of the female sub-sample indicated that the husband was the only provider of income in the household. 62% of the male sub-sample, contrasted with 80.2% of the female, indicated that the wife was basically responsible for the care of the children.

Delegating responsibility of caring for children to elder sons or male members of the household, especially when the husband is absent, is also a common practice on the West Bank. A parallel study conducted in East Jordan noted that, whilst the above practice was also common with the sons, it was not as far as the daughters were concerned.[1] Instead, the mother shared the responsibility of caring for them with the elder daughters.

With regard to disciplining children, parents have never delegated such responsibility to outsiders, such as teachers and others. This practice is also extended to elder sons who reside in their parents' home, in that they continue to be under at least the verbal discipline of their parents.[2]

The results in Tables I and II show that 66% of the male sub-sample and 41% of the female sub-sample indicated that the husband and wife, jointly, discipline their children, whereas more than twice as many females (38.3%) as males (15%) indicated that they are basically in charge of discipline of their children.

The majority of the two sub-samples indicated that the kinship role is performed jointly. Of the female sub-sample (Table III) 56.6% and 57% of the male sub-sample (Table I) indicated that the husband and the wife jointly plan visits to and contact with their relatives, and 50.3% of the female sub-sample and 57% of the male sub-sample indicated that they jointly organised family entertainment and recreation.

Interestingly, the ratio of the male sub-sample (Table I) who indicated that the husband is basically responsible for family entertainment (30%) is almost triple that of the female sub-sample

[1] Basson, P. *op. cit.* (p.53).
[2] *ibid.* (p.31).

(Table III) who indicated the opposite (13.7%). The same is also true regarding visiting relatives with the percentage of responses being 20% males and 9% females.

As regards cleaning of the house, 87% of the male sub-sample indicated that their wives are basically in charge of it. (Table I), and 88.7% of the female sub-sample indicated that they are actually in charge (Table III).

Having introduced a background of comparative analysis between the male and female sub-samples, it would be appropriate to make an observation of Basson's study, before analysing the responses of the three age groups. Basson[3] found that the best way to get around the subjective interpretation of the meaning of decision maker, a phrase which invites a variety of definitions, was to adopt the most common local definition; the decision maker is 'the main responsible'.

For example, the question of 'do you receive any help in disciplining your children?', usually attracts some sort of response. If, however, the question is altered into, 'who is responsible for disciplining the children?', fewer subjects would give a definite answer, opting instead for a shared responsibility in disciplining children, usually with other members of the extended family.

As regards the possible differences in the ratio of responses between the three age groups, most responses are eliminated in favour of only two: either, only/mostly the husband or, jointly, husband and wife.

The latter category accommodated responses involving the slightest contribution by either spouse to a joint decision making, as it involved a certain degree of interaction away from a one-sided, autocratic stance. In so doing, one can determine the extent to which women's roles have become supportive, complementary or simply did not change at all. One can also determine whether women are now allowed to participate fully in various societal responsibilities, without compromising their dedication to 'honour'. In addition, it would be possible to find out what new roles women have taken and to what degree they are inconsistent with their traditional ones; that is, if they are undergoing a period of reappraisal and readjustment.

In order to test for any significant variability in means of responses amongst the three age groups, the analysis of variance

[3] Basson, P. *op. cit.* (p.30).

(*t*-test) was employed twice for each of the indicators. The first five tables reflect the results of the following questions. 'In your current marital life, who is (mainly) responsible for the following?'

The six tables which follow them reflect the results of the question 'In an *ideal* situation who, in your opinion should be (mainly) responsible for the following?'.

a: Division of Labour

Table V. *Sample Responses to the Question: 'In your current marital life, who is mainly responsible for providing income?' (three age groups)*

Age group	Responses: Only/mainly husband	Jointly/ husband and wife	Total
1. 'Young' (M1)	343	32	375
2. 'Middle-age' (M2)	348	72	420
3. 'Old' (M3)	89	15	104
			899

$f = 0.491$; $f<F\,(0.95, 2, 3) = 9.55$; $0.491<9.55$
Accept H_0
Kendall's Tau, $C = 0.08566$; Significance = 0.00
Gamma = 0.31944

The results given in the *t*-test clearly indicate that there are no significant differences in the mean squares of the responses amongst the three generations. In other words, the ratios of the responses (or attitudes) towards employment amongst the different age groups are not statistically different – there is no significant shift in the employment pattern.

Here, the concept of honour is closely related to the division of space and labour. Traditionally, labour by women in a mixed environment outside the household was the exception and not the rule. The reason behind this was that the violation of the 'male' space outside the house is an infringement of the honour. Indeed, the house and any domestic activities related to the house, are considered feminine and private; streets, markets, cafés and mosques are all considered masculine and public.

In his 1978 study, Takla[4] found no relation between sex role attitudes and career aspirations between working and non-working women. He concluded that women's employment does not necessarily evoke liberalised attitudes from other members of both the family and the community towards the woman's role in the family. That is, maternal employment by itself does not reflect change in a husband dominated family structure.

Another reason why the role of the wife continues to be domesticated and the women's forces have not increased as anticipated across the three age groups can be explained by the following: menial tasks are still considered degrading by middle and upper-class women, and to a lesser extent men. It is for this reason that college girls, for example, from these classes in the four main universities, would never take jobs as shop assistants, hygiene instructors in refugee camps, waitresses and so on. Alternatives in employment, to lower class wives, are obviously limited by their low level of education. One would, therefore, expect their work to be domestic or home-oriented. And it is not uncommon for those who are uneducated to seek one or two days a week as 'domestic assistants' in middle or upper class households.

A comparative remark is quite befitting here. In her study of East Jordanian women, Basson notes that they are still regarded with suspicion if they are employed in the public sphere. In addition 'she has two full-time jobs, one as a wage earner and one as home-maker. Her entry into the public sphere is not matched by a corresponding entry of her husband into the private sphere of the home-making and child care. Her home-making activities are conducted in a manner of keeping up with day to day demands'.[5]

Though the latter part of the observation can be generalised to be also true of the West Bank, the basic social, economic and political realities within the nature of division of labour must be regarded at variance between West Bankers and East Jordanians. The traditional practice by village women, for example, of marketing their harvests in close-by Arab markets in West Bank townships, has not disappeared. There has been a slight change, however, regarding male labourers in the Israeli economy who have their day off on Saturday, this being the religious Jewish day instead of Friday, for Moslems.

[4] Takla, S. M.A. thesis, *op. cit.*, 1978.

[5] Basson, P. *op. cit.* (p.66).

In order to find out what shifts, if any, exist in regards to future aspirations towards the division of labour (income) the following question was asked: 'In an *ideal* situation, who, in your opinion should be (mainly) responsible for income?'

The results are quite interesting and consistent with our expectations.

In the first instance, the null hypothesis indicating that the mean squares of responses between the three age groups are *not* significant, was accepted. That is, the ratios of answers amongst the three age groups are uniform (Table VI).

Table VI. *Sample Response to the Question: 'In an* ideal *situation, who, in your opinion, should be mainly responsible for providing income?' (three age groups)*

Age group	*Only/mainly husband*	*Jointly husband and wife*	*Total*
1. Young (M1)	217	150	367
2. Middle-age (M2)	252	155	407
3. Old (M3)	85	26	111
			885

$f = 4.45$; $f<F$ $(0.95, 2, 3) = 955$; $4.45<9.55$
Accept H_0
Kendall's Tau $C = 0.05532$; Significance $= 0.01$
Gamma $= 0.1163$

Secondly, at the 0.001 level of the significance (Kendall's Tau *C* test), the level of association between the two main variables are statistical. That is, there is a greater tendency amongst younger age groups to aspire to a joint role between the spouses to bring income home. Almost half (150 of 367) of the 'young' age group, as compared with a quarter (26 of 111) of 'old' age group aspire for both spouse to earn income, in an *ideal* circumstance.

Yet, the shift in responses between Tables V and VI for the three age groups are also significant according to the Chi-square test (see Table VII).

The results are somewhat encouraging, in that a sizeable percentage aspire for a joint participation in income responsibilities and financial burdens, which explains why a rigid division of

Table VII. *χ^2 test of Tables V and VI*

	Table V				Table VI				ΣTable V / ΣTable VI		
	Husband	Husband and wife	Total		Husband	Husband and wife	Total		Husband	Husband and wife	Total
M1	343	32	375	M1	217	150	367	M1	220.43	152.37	372.80
M2	348	72	420	M2	252	155	407	M2	255.99	157.45	413.44
M3	89	15	104	M3	85	26	111	M3	86.34	26.41	112.75
			889				885				898.99

$\chi^2_2 = 247.7$
$\chi^2 > \chi_2\ (2,\ 0.95) = 5.991$
Reject H_0 (differences are significant)

labour is circumstantial, and is kept going by restrictions imposed by the society.

The issue of concern, then, is how much of the domesticated role of women is induced by the belief that wage-orientated labour in the public sphere is unnecessary and immoral, and, to what extent do sex roles add up to the current religio-cultural restrictions in bringing about the confinement of women's duties to their home.

And, finally, any increase in the proportion of women in the labour force is uniquely intrinsic to the pace of the growth and development of institutions on the West Bank, be they educational, health oriented, social welfare or other civic responsibilities. Obviously, an actual growth in the industry is but one factor towards encouraging women to participate in the labour force. Yet, a state of non-growth should not hinder women from moving into traditionally male-dominated occupations, provided of course that the males' level of objection is not as constraining as it used to be.

Expressions of such attitudes can only be considered as signs opposed to a change in the status of women. Emancipation of 'females' would then be under the category of 'superficial', not 'essential' changes.

All the same, since the establishment of the four Palestinian universities in the aftermath of the Israeli invasion in 1967, mixing in the classroom and outside it became a fact of life. For the first time, we notice that the active involvement of females in the organisation of national movements and activities admitting, however, that the Western practice of dating outside the university walls is still a very rare event.

b: Sex-Role Activities

There have been numerous discussions on sex-roles and behaviour prescribed to each of the sexes in Middle Eastern communities by social scientists and others. Each of the sex roles was nurtured, and as a result functions only in a social world that is distinct from other ones. Hence, the women's world has been described as 'private' and the man's as 'public'.[6] The private world is domestic,

6 Marx, E. *Bedouin of the Negev*, New York, Praeger, 1967; Peters, E. *Consequences of the Segregation of the Sexes among the Arabs* (paper given at Mediterranean Social Science Council Conferences, Athens, 1966).

confined and housebound involving 'feminine duties': the public world involves the man in a wide range of duties and authority.

Traditionally, polarisation of the sexes has been precipitated by codes of honour and modesty in the majority of Middle Eastern Arab cultures. Characteristics and behaviour of the sexes have thus become interwoven, and can be easily observed in the local West Bank society. (Antoun, 1969; Dodd, 1970 and 1973.)

Subsequently, any changes in the woman's behaviour is the result of changing definitions of the codes of modesty and honour by the society itself.

The division between the sexes is expressed cogently, albeit in an observation that is related to the man, in the following:

> "The men's world has two major manifestations: the sphere of earning a living and the public sphere of communications, including public affairs. Access of women to the former is limited and is formally none in the latter. No doubt that the two worlds have their regular meeting point at home, for this is where a good deal of clearing goes on continuously'.[7]

Though the description above deals with Arab cultures in general, and the information is somewhat backdated, it is informative to a certain degree about the women's social life as depicted by a Western male anthropologist. We have, in fact, formulated a few questions to test if such polarisation between Palestinian sexes does emerge; and what they perceived, were the significant aspects of an *ideal* role in the future.

c: Child Care Role

Wives continue to be very active with regards to caring for their children.

Indeed, the ratio of wives who indicated that they are responsible for caring for their children is fivefold (at 670) that of a 'joint' (husband and wife) responsibility (at 147). The ratio, however, drops from five to three when the sample was asked about their aspiration in an *ideal* situation (Table IX). There were 509 responses favouring the wife to be in charge of caring for her children, as opposed to 342 who favoured a 'joint' (husband and wife) responsibility.

[7] Nieuwenliujze, C. von *Social Stratification in the Middle East*, The Hague, E. Brill, 1965.

Table VIII. *Sample Response to the Question 'In your current marital life, who is mainly responsible for caring for children?' (three age groups)*

Age group	*Only/mainly wife*	*Jointly wife and husband*	*Total*
1. Young	267	53	320
2. Middle-age	321	72	393
3. Old	32	22	104
	670	147	885

$f = 0.68$; $f<F\ (0.95, 2, 3) = 9.95$; $0.68<9.55$
Accept H_0
Kendall's Tau $C = 0.04591$; Significance $= 0.02$
Gamma $= 0.1063$

Table IX. *Sample Responses to the Question: 'In an* ideal *situation, who, in your opinion, should be mainly responsible for caring for children?' (three age groups)*

Age group	*Only/mainly wife*	*Jointly wife and husband*	*Total*
1. Young	185	172	357
2. Middle-age	251	134	385
3. Old	73	36	109
	509	342	851

$f = 4.55$; $f<F\ (0.95, 2, 3) = 9.95$; $4.55<9.55$
Accept H_0
Kendall's Tau $C = 0.08215$; Significance $= 0.001$
Gamma $= 0.1603$

Interestingly, results obtained in the *t*-test indicate that the mean squares of the responses between the three age groups are consistent. That is, given that the null hypothesis is accepted, any observable differences between the three age groups are due to chance.

Yet, some of the most encouraging findings are those obtained by employing the Chi-square test, to see if there are significant differences in the results between Tables VIII and IX. Table X

Table X. *χ^2 test of Tables VIII and IX*

	Table VIII				*Table IX*				*ΣTable XIII*		
									ΣTable IX		
	Wife	*Wife and husband*	*Total*		*Wife*	*Wife and husband*	*Total*		*Wife*	*Wife and husband*	*Total*
M1	267	53	320	M1	185	172	357	M1	177.61	165.13	342.74
M2	321	72	393	M2	251	134	385	M2	240.97	128.65	369.62
M3	82	22	104	M3	73	36	109	M3	70.08	34.56	104.64
			817				851				817.00

$\chi^2 = 179.30$
$\chi^2 > \chi^2\ (2, 0.95) = 5.991$
Reject H_0 (differences are significant)

indicates that the differences in responses between the two tables are real. That is, there is a definite increase in the percentage of individuals who indicated that the responsibility of caring for children should be jointly adopted.

ii: Housekeeping Role

Cleaning the house and other domestic affairs continues to be predominantly the domain of the wife across the three age groups. A majority of 829 respondents indicated that house cleaning is a role that is primarily that of the wife; as opposed to only 31 who indicated that it is a joint (husband and wife) role (Table XI).

As regards the shift in the mean square of responses amongst the three age groups, results obtained from the analysis of variance (t-test) indicated that it is not significant.

Table XI. *Sample Response to the Question: 'In your current marital life, who is mainly responsible for cleaning the house?' (three age groups)*

Age group	*Only/mainly wife*	*Jointly husband and wife*	*Total*
1. Young	344	17	361
2. Middle-age	381	10	391
3. Old	104	4	108
	829	31	860

$f = 0.09$
Accept H_0: $f<F$ (0.95, 2, 3) = 9.95; 0.09<9.55
Kendall's Tau C = 0.00007; Significance = 0.49
Gamma = 0.00034

Results obtained in Table XII also show that though the number of respondents who think that house cleaning should be a shared activity in an *ideal* situation has increased slightly, the ratio between the mean squares amongst the three age groups is consistent. In other words, the null hypothesis is accepted, since any perceived differences between the mean squares amongst the three age groups are due to chance.

Noteworthy is that the 0.49 (Table XI) and 0.07 (Table XII) level of significance, any perceived differences between the two variables: age groups and the given responses, are due to chance.

Table XII. *Sample Responses to the Question: 'In an* ideal *situation, who, in your opinion, should be mainly responsible for cleaning the house?' (three age groups)*

Age group	*Only/mainly wife*	*Jointly wife and husband*	*Total*
1. Young	284	59	343
2. Middle-age	332	53	385
3. Old	95	16	111
	711	128	839

$f = 0.48$; $f<F\ (0.95, 2, 3) = 9.95$
Accept H_0; $0.48<9.55$
Kendall's Tau $C = 0.03230$; Significance $= 0.07$
Gamma $= 0.08998$

Table XIII, however, indicates a real difference in the results between the two tables, XI and XII. The significant changes can be viewed as encouraging signs in that the present unilateral role of house cleaning for the West Bank women at present is *de facto*, not *de jure*. It seems as though for one reason or another there are fewer individuals who wished that house cleaning duties, like 'income' and 'care of children' were distributed more equally between the sexes.

iii: Discipline of Children

Disciplining children involves socialising children into acceptable behaviour, attending to school problems, and so on.

Figures obtained from Table XIV show that there are twice the number of spouses 'jointly' involved in the discipline of their children across the three age groups than there are wives 'single-handedly' performing these duties. Results obtained in the *t*-test show that there are no significant differences in the ratio of responses across the three generations for both tables, XIV and XV.

Although the perceived ratios in response between the three age groups appear inconsistent (Table XV) in that there are almost four times as many youngsters (M1) who aspire for a 'joint' role in disciplining children compared with a ratio of two to one amongst the 'old' (M3), the differences in the ratio are not significant.

The level of significance in Kendall's Tau *C*, however, suggests a strong relationship between the two main variables in both Tables

Table XIII. χ^2 *of Tables XI and XII*

	Table XI				*Table XII*				*ΣTable XI / ΣTable XII*		
	Wife	*Wife and husband*	*Total*		*Wife*	*Wife and husband*	*Total*		*Wife*	*Wife and husband*	*Total*
M1	344	17	361	M1	384	59	343	M1	291.1	60.48	351.58
M2	381	10	391	M2	332	53	385	M2	340.3	45.3	385.6
M3	104	4	108	M3	95	16	111	M3	97.3	16.4	113.7
			860				839				850.88

$\chi^2 = 91.73$
$\chi^2 > \chi^2$ (2, 0.95) = 5.991
Reject H_0 (differences are significant)

XIV (significance = 0.02) and XV (significance = 0.005). It follows that there is a tendency for the young age group to prefer to act 'jointly' when it comes to disciplining their children rather than letting the wife do it on her own.

Table XIV. *Sample Responses to the Question: 'In your current marital life, who is mainly responsible for disciplining children?' (three age groups)*

Age group	*Only/mainly wife*	*Jointly wife and husband*	*Total*
1. Young	101	205	306
2. Middle-age	118	231	349
3. Old	40	60	100

$f = 2.216$; $F<f\ (0.92, 2, 3) = 9.95$; $2.216<9.55$
Accept H_0
Kendall's Tau $C = -0.0556$; Significance = 0.02
Gamma = −0.09688

Table XV. *Sample Responses to the Question: 'In an* ideal *situation, who, in your opinion, should be mainly responsible for disciplining children?' (three age groups)*

Age group	*Only/mainly wife*	*Jointly wife and husband*	*Total*
1. Young	70	282	352
2. Middle-age	105	279	384
3. Old	38	68	107

An analysis of results in Table XVI supports our expectations: that there is a real shift in the overall responses between Tables XIV and XV towards an increase in a joint role (played by both spouses) regarding disciplining their children, should societal circumstances change in the future.

It would also be interesting for a future analysis to find out whether the temporary emigration of the household head (husband) has an impact in authority (decision making) and structural organisation of the family.

Table XVI. χ^2 *of Tables XIV and XV*

	Table XIV				*Table XV*				*ΣTable XIV / ΣTable XV*		
	Wife	*Wife and husband*	*Total*		*Wife*	*Wife and husband*	*Total*		*Wife*	*Wife and husband*	*Total*
M1	101	205	306	M1	70	282	352	M1	62.69	252.56	315.25
M2	118	231	349	M2	105	279	384	M2	94.04	249.88	343.92
M3	40	60	100	M3	38	68	107	M3	34.03	60.9	94.93
			755				843				754.1

$\chi^2 = 40.96$
$\chi^2 > \chi^2\ (2, 0.95) = 5.991$
Reject H_0 (differences are significant)

iv: Kinship Role

The kinship role involves responsibility for family entertainment, and contact with or visits to relatives.

Since the Israeli occupation of the West Bank in 1967, the social life there has generally been sterile, due to the curbing of social and cultural associations and clubs, and the nagging security patrols and checkpoints during night hours.

The absence of structural collective social activities ultimately reduced a sizeable number of people into a routine of playing cards in cafés, brooding about possibilities of migrating and visiting acquaintances during the daytime.

Going to the cinema has been restricted to trickles of male teenagers trying to alleviate boredom, and most importantly because of the absence of Jordanian censorship on morally loose films. Meanwhile, television sets became common gathering points in the evening for family members.

It would seem that the combined forces of day-to-day cultural practices as affected by the instability of the area and decisions of Israeli authorities, contributed to the social state of affairs. For instance, indulging in luxurious idleness by talking about the slightest changes in their lives or those of their acquaintances, or the lack of it, whilst knitting sweaters, playing with rosary beads or simply eating assortments of nuts, is a well cherished pastime. One of the sample interviewees was quoted directly as saying; 'the topics people talk about are so narrow and limited . . . How long are the eyelashes of the daughter of this and that . . . How *ibin* such and such used to walk so many kilos (kilometres) surviving on two olives and a tomato' and so on.

An apt remark here is that the polarised sex roles have in certain circumstances given Palestinian women an advantage over men.

The conical role which the Arab (Palestinian) woman was observed to play has been one of linking various members of the extended family with one another. Functions of such a role are illustrated in detail in many literary studies:

> "The woman as a daughter, sister, wife, and mother acts as an 'information broker', mediating social relations within the family and larger society. The implications for power (reciprocity of influences) are obvious in that by these networks of relationships, the woman is in a position to channel or withhold information to the male members of the

kindred. And in this position the woman influences decision making about alliances; actually sets up marriage conditions and informs male members of the household what is going on in other homes."[8]

Listing these observations is, of course, not exclusive to the polarised roles amongst Arab Palestinian women. The on-going debates in Western societies regarding disparity in salaries between the sexes, alternative life-styles and conflicting occupational roles are all indicative of a similar syndrome; not to mention the possibility of it being a universal one.

The results in Table XVII show the extent to which making an active decision about entertaining the household members revolves around 'either' or 'joint' sex roles. The ratio of both spouses taking a 'joint' decision regarding family entertainment is higher for all age groups than that of the husbands making the decision by themselves. Analysis of variance, however, indicates that there are no changes in the mean responses amongst the different age groups – the differences in the responses are uniform.

Table XVII. *Sample Responses to the Question: 'In your current marital life, who is mainly responsible for family entertainment?' (three age groups)*

Age group	*Only/mainly husband*	*Jointly husband and wife*	*Total*
1. Young	122	188	310
2. Middle-age	138	190	328
3. Old	38	52	90
	298	430	728

$f = 7.28$; $f < F\ (00.95, 2, 3) = 9.95$; $7.28 < 9.55$
Accept H_0
Kendall's Tau $C = 0.02706$; Significance = 0.168
Gamma = 0.04203

8 Nelson, C. 'Public and private politics: women in the Middle Eastern world' in *Arab Society in Transition, ed.* Ibrahim, S., Cairo, American University, 1977 (p.142).

Table XVIII. *Sample Responses to the Question: 'In an* ideal *situation, who, in your opinion, should be mainly responsible for family entertainment?' (three age groups)*

Age group	*Only/mainly husband*	*Jointly husband and wife*	*Total*
1. Young	98	237	335
2. Middle-age	112	245	257
3. Old	34	67	101
	244	549	793

$f = 1.6$; $f<F$ (0.95, 2, 3) = 9.95; 1.6<9.55
Accept H_0
Kendall's Tau C = 0.00568; Significance = 0.41
Gamma = 0.01057

Illustrated in Table XVIII are responses which are comparatively more clustered around a (husband and wife) 'joint' decision than the previous Table (XVII) when it comes to expressing one's aspirations about family entertainment in 'more favourable' circumstances; *i.e. ideal* ones.

Analysis of variance in the *t*-test indicates that there are no significant differences in the mean responses across the three age groups, *i.e.* whatever changes are perceived are not real but are due to chance.

Like the previous table, the level of significance (at 0.4 level) for the current table (XVII) confirms that there is no relationship of significance between the two variables: age category and a 'joint' democratic-like decision about family entertainment.

Figures illustrated above are consistent with our hypothesis – that there is a significant shift in response between the two tables, XVII and XVIII. That is, given an appropriate cultural environment, a liberal attitude reflecting a democratic joint decision towards entertaining family members would follow.

Responses as to which spouse is at present responsible for contact and arrangement of visit of relatives (and friends) are uniformly polarised across the three age groups. Results obtained in Table XX show that the ratio of responses across the three age groups are not significant; that there is no shift in the mean responses between one group and another.

Table XIX. χ^2 *test of Tables XVII and XVIII*

	Table XVII				*Table XVIII*				*ΣTable XVII / ΣTable XVIII*		
	Husband	*Husband and wife*	*Total*		*Husband*	*Husband and wife*	*Total*		*Husband*	*Husband and wife*	*Total*
M1	122	188	310	M1	98	237	335	M1	89.97	217.57	307.54
M2	138	190	328	M2	112	245	357	M2	102.82	224.92	327.74
M3	38	52	90	M3	34	67	101	M3	31.21	61.51	92.72
			728				793				728.00

$\chi^2 = 35.83$
$\chi^2 > \chi^2\ (2, 0.95) = 5.991$
Reject H_0 (differences are significant)

The direction of these results also indicates that there are approximately three times the number of 'both' spouses undertaking a joint decision in making contacts with relatives and friends as there are husbands taking this decision on his own. It would seem that maintaining a relationship with one's friends and relatives is not manipulated solely by either spouse. This is also consistent across age groups as the relationship between the two variables: 'differences in age' and a 'joint' democratic decision regarding visits of relatives and friends, is not significant (significance = 0.09).

Table XX. *Sample Responses to the Question: 'In your current marital life, who is mainly responsible for making contacts/visiting relatives/friends?' (three age groups)*

Age group	*Only/mainly husband*	*Jointly husband and wife*	*Total*
1. Young	78	220	298
2. Middle-age	81	236	317
3. Old	23	64	83
	182	520	720

$f = 1.07$; $f < F$ (0.95, 2, 3) = 9.95; 1.07<9.55
Accept H_0 (Null hypothesis)
Kendall's Tau C = 0.03546; Significance = 0.09
Gamma = 0.06149

Similar to the results found in Table XX there is no significant inconsistency in the mean responses across the three age groups regarding an envisaged preferred role in the future (Table XXI). The gap between the two responses: 'mainly husband' and 'jointly' husband and wife, has widened; but given the results in the *t*-test, the ratio between the two responses are uniform and consistent; not indicating a shift across the three age groups (significance = 0.23).

One minor interesting change has unexpectedly occurred with regard to responses of the 'old' age groups as seen in Table XX and XXI. There are actually more 'old' respondents (at 27) who favour husbands taking on the sole responsibility of contacting relatives in an *ideal* situation than those indicating the same response at *present* (at 23).

Table XXI. *Sample Responses to the Question: 'In an* ideal *situation, who, in your opinion, should be mainly responsible for contacting/visiting relatives/friends?' (three age groups)*

Age group	*Only/mainly husband*	*Jointly husband and wife*	*Total*
1. Young	58	260	318
2. Middle-age	66	285	351
3. Old	27	70	97
	151	615	766

$f = 0.63$; $f < F\ (0.95, 2, 3) = 9.95$; $0.63 < 9.55$
Accept H_0
Kendall's Tau $C = 0.01778$; Significance = 0.23
Gamma = −0.03731

The overall results in the previous two tables show a significant change has taken place, as indicated in the Chi-square test (Table XXIII); that is, there is a statistical change in the overall responses between the current responsibilities of visiting relatives/friends and what is thought to be the *ideal* situation.

In order to measure the extent of the male's overall dominance in decision making, the same previous indicator was employed, but in a different form. Thus the following question was formulated: 'Who is the primary force behind the current distribution of responsibilities regarding a) income, b) child care, c) cleaning of house, d) discipline of children, e) family entertainment and f) visits and contact with relatives'.

Results obtained in the following three tables clearly show that the decisions behind the present distribution of the first three roles, a), b) and c), were predominantly 'unilateral'. To illustrate, the proportion of joint decisions behind the current role of providing income is almost one fifth of that of a unilateral decision by the husband. A similar proportion is reflected in the second role area. There are 178 respondents indicating that there was a joint decision behind the present distribution of 'care of children', as opposed to 580 where the decision was taken unilaterally by the wife.

As regards 'cleaning of the house' the proportion of a unilateral decision; namely the wife's, is much higher (at 724 responses) than that taken 'jointly', by both spouses (at 80 responses).

Table XXII. *χ^2 Test of Tables XX and XXI*

	Table XX				*Table XXI*				*ΣTable XX* / *ΣTable XXI*		
	Husband	*Husband and wife*	*Total*		*Husband*	*Husband and wife*	*Total*		*Husband*	*Husband and wife*	*Total*
M1	78	220	298	M1	58	260	318	M1	53.51	238.28	291.79
M2	81	236	317	M2	66	285	351	M2	60.49	261.19	321.68
M3	23	64	87	M3	27	70	97	M3	24.74	64.15	88.89
			702				766				702.36

$\chi^2 = 22.53$
$\chi^2 > \chi^2\ (2, 0.95) = 5.991$
Reject H_0 (differences are significant)

Results obtained in the *t*-test support the contention that there are no significant differences in the response means across the three age groups.

Table XXIII. *Responses to the Question: 'Who is the primary force behind the* current *distribution of responsibilities regarding 'income'?' (three age groups)*

Age group	*Only/mainly husband*	*Jointly husband and wife*	*Total*
1. Young	283	45	328
2. Middle-age	311	64	375
3. Old	79	16	95
	673	125	

$f = 0.554$; $f<F\ (0.95, 2, 3) = 9.95$; $0.55<9.55$
Accept H_0
Kendall's Tau $C = 0.02851$; Significance = 0.11
Gamma = 0.06721

Table XXIV. *Responses to the Question: 'Who is the primary force behind the* current *distribution of responsibilities regarding 'care of children'?' (three age groups)*

Age group	*Only/mainly wife*	*Jointly wife and husband*	*Total*
1. Young	217	73	290
2. Middle-age	289	82	371
3. Old	74	23	97
	580	178	750

$f = 0.896$; $f<F\ (0.95, 2, 3) = 9.95$; $0.89<9.55$
Accept H_0
Kendall's Tau $C = 0.0782$; Significance = 0.002
Gamma = 0.129

The direction of the results for the remaining three tables are almost the opposite to the last three. Thus, the proportion of a 'joint-decision' (both spouses) behind the present distribution of duties regarding e), f) and g) is greater than that taken 'unilaterally' by the husband or wife alone (Tables XXVI, XXVII and XXVIII).

Table XXV. *Responses to the Question: 'Who is the primary force behind the* current *distribution of responsibilities regarding 'cleaning the house'?' (three age groups)*

Age group	*Only/mainly wife*	*Jointly wife and husband*	*Total*
1. Young	283	37	320
2. Middle-age	347	36	383
3. Old	94	7	101
	724	80	804

$f = 0.39$; $f<F$ (0.95, 2, 3) = 9.95; 0.39<9.55
Accept H_0
Kendall's Tau C = 0.0504; Significance = 0.02
Gamma = 0.1107

Apart from Table XXVII, results obtained in the *t*-test indicate that the mean square of responses for the three age groups are not significantly different; *i.e.* any perceived changes are consistent and uniform.

Table XXVII indicates that the null hypotheses must be rejected with reference to the results obtained in the *t*-test, but only with regards to the 'middle-age' and 'old' groups. The mean squares of responses between the above groups are significantly different. The direction of responses between the two groups are clearly

Table XXVI. *Responses to the Question: 'Who is the primary force behind the* current *distribution of responsibilities regarding 'discipline of the children'?' (three age groups)*

Age group	*Only/mainly wife*	*Jointly wife and husband*	*Total*
1. Young	110	178	288
2. Middle-age	147	221	368
3. Old	40	56	96
	297	455	752

$f = 5.7$; $f<F$ (0.95, 2, 3) = 9.95; 5.7<9.55
Accept H_0
Kendall's Tau C = 0.08105; Significance = 0.001
Gamma = 0.130

opposite to one another. The proportion of those who took a 'joint' decision amongst the 'old' group in the entertainment of the family is greater than the proportion in which the husband made the decision alone. The result is opposite to the result for the 'middle-age' group.

Table XXVII. *Responses to the Question: 'Who is the primary force behind the* current *distribution of responsibilities regarding 'family entertainment?' (three age groups)*

Age group	Only/mainly husband	Jointly husband and wife	Total
(M1) 1. Young	136	151	287
(M2) 2. Middle-age	139	191	330
(M3) 3. Old	41	50	91
	316	392	708

$f = 16.2$; $f > F\ (0.95, 2, 3) = 9.95$; $16.2 > 9.55$
Reject H_0 ($M2 \neq M3$) = ($M2 < M3$)
($t = 5.33$; $5.33 > 4.51$)
Kendall's Tau $C = 0.008$; Significance = 0.37
Gamma = 0.013

Table XXVIII. *Responses to the Question: 'Who is the primary force behind the* current *distribution of responsibilities regarding 'visits with relatives'?' (three age groups)*

Age group	Only/mainly husband	Jointly husband and wife	Total
1. Young	124	160	284
2. Middle-age	115	219	334
3. Old	34	48	82
	273	427	700

$f = 2.82$; $f < F\ (0.95, 2, 3) = 9.95$; $2.82 < 9.55$
Accept H_0
Kendall's Tau $C = 0.0088$; Significance = 0.37
Gamma = 0.032

Conclusion

It has been contended that structural organisation of kinship systems on the West Bank tends to affect sentiments and attitudes and to mould certain social and sexual roles amongst family members. Indeed, the polarisation of sex roles for the whole Arab Middle Eastern region is so fixed that it acquired the term 'male vanity culture'.[9]

Six variables were introduced in order to tap any possible differences in authority structure and decision making processes between the two sexes and across the three age groups.

The six variables, which were selected in order to measure and analyse which of the two sexes and age groups were more active in decision making, were:

a) provision of income, b) care of children,
c) cleaning of house, d) discipline of children,
e) family entertainment, f) visits and contact with relatives.

The analysis of variance in the *t*-test was employed in order to detect any possible statistical changes in responses across the different groups.

Further, in order to speculate about the future, despite the scarcity of statistics on this subject matter, another indicator was introduced. The subjects were asked to speculate about distribution of duties according to sex roles in an ideal situation.

With regards to all of the six indices employed, no consistent differences in the means of responses were noted amongst the three age categories. The income provider was predominantly the male. Conversely, the majority of the three age groups uniformly indicated that care of children and house cleaning were two domestic roles for which the wife alone is responsible.

As regards the three remaining measures, the ratio of a shared responsibility was almost twice that of an individual one. Thus, two-thirds of the responses indicated that both spouses were responsible for disciplining their children compared with one-third indicating that the wife alone was responsible. A similar ratio was obtained regarding family entertainment with one-third indicating the husband; and the same also regarding making family contacts and visits, with one-third indicating the husband.

[9] Riesman, D. *The Lonely Crowd*, 1950.

Results obtained as to who was the primary force behind the present distribution of duties or roles match the researchers' expectations. Ratios obtained in the previous analysis again reflect themselves in the same manner on this indicator. The mean responses across the three age groups were uniform, reflecting no statistical differences, except for family entertainment (Table XXVII). It is indicated that the proportion of those who took a joint decision about entertainment of the family is greater than the proportion of males who made the decisions alone in the case of the 'old' group. This is opposite to the responses of the middle-aged group.

The most interesting results obtained are those in response to a preferred role, given appropriate circumstances and an *ideal* society. Though none of the differences in the mean responses across the three age groups is significant, the overall direction of the responses has changed. Specifically the proportion of those preferring a shared responsibility in domestic and non-domestic roles across the three generations has, in some indicators, more than doubled.

The overall changes between the present roles and the preferred future role regarding the six indicators were statistically significant, employing the Chi-square test.

It would seem that clinging to traditional, sex-prescribed roles is perpetuated by impulses of imminent danger that the family unit might collapse. Fear of deviation from a rigid sex-role polarised society adds another dimension to this situation.

Being a part of a larger community of traditional Arab women, West Bank women find that accepting roles and statuses prescribed to them by tradition is a natural state of events. During the sequence of interviewing, a woman cited verses from the Koran that, 'if we behave like our men we will never be happy one centimetre (sic) because we will never be happy' (interview 170).

It would seem right to believe that men and women who are little touched by the modern world should insist upon maintaining traditional roles and duties which have been rigidly conscripted.

Precisely because the honour of the male depends on the woman's social conduct, men are highly suspicious of women in this sphere.

According to the Al-Khawli[10] and other Arab and Moslem

[10] Al-Khawli, Al Bahi, *Al-Mara bein al-Beit wal Mujtana* (Women Between the Home and Society) Cairo, 1960 (p.45).

scholars, nature or destiny is responsible for the division of labour between the two sexes. By this, he emphatically refers to the *burdensome repercussions* of pregnancy, which limit both of the women's mental and physical capacities. This complaint that equalisation of the sexes will 'defeminise' women is vaguely argued along the lines that differences of superiority are brought about by the requirements of reality.[11]

Such exploitative attitudes, assumptions and impositions of unfair values are uniformly ingrained in all Arab Moslem societies, in varying degrees, including on the West Bank. The only exception being the unique political development and resultant unstable developments on the West Bank, which inadvertently affected all aspects of Palestinian culture.

Though conservatives have submitted to a *fait accompli* position, a sizeable proportion of the sample contends that, were conditions on the West Bank different, power structure in the family would change towards equality. For instance, the theme of freedom is expressed by a young refugee woman, with a high school certificate:

> "In countries of the West, you can go to cultural places of fine arts and music, films and learn dancing. Don't you think we like this too! God will change all this some day."

A minority in the sample which reflects such aspirations displays a certain feeling of ambivalence; thus, whilst they like to change facets of their life, they are not certain about how comfortable they will be. In a succinct uttering, a middle-aged interviewee rationalises: 'more freedom causes more insecurity'.

Whatever reasons are given towards adopting certain attitudes, shaped by social traditions, one thing seems certain: as Palestinian youths, particularly from Jerusalem, are exposed to new pleasures and desires of the Israeli culture, their assumptions and definitions will deviate from the norm.

Goode[12] remarked in 1963 that changes, in general, do bring with them a certain degree of frustration, yet change is welcome because it brings with it freedom of choice and an increase in the available options.

[11] *ibid*. (p.46).
[12] Goode, W. *op. cit.*, 1963.

One would also have argued if the desires and expressions of Palestinian youngsters continue to grow beyond the shock which the culture is equipped to absorb, a state of psychosocial disruptions will develop. Part of these disruptions are, of course, interfamilial relationships – a topic which will be analysed in the forthcoming chapter.

Chapter VII

Marital Adjustment, Dynamics and Interrelationships

Introduction

Kinship loyalty ranks as a paramount virtue amongst West Bank Palestinians, the same way that it does in other Middle Eastern societies. Individuals tend to submit to an eventual reliance on and support from the extended family, at least in times of crisis.

Obviously, the emotional cost becomes considerable as members of the family utilise opportunities for requesting favours to be reciprocated.

Although it is argued that the nuclear family is an emergency trend on the West Bank, and that brothers and sisters have for one reason or another become geographically distant, obligations, personal contact and familial network functions continue to be the same.

Gullic's illustration of this point of the Arab culture in general is apt here, he notes:

> "The conventional expectations of the Arab culture generally are that adult brothers will remain in contact with each other and be mentally loyal and helpful, throughout life.
>
> The conventional expectations of brother–sister relationships are a little more complex. As long as she is unmarried, a girl or young woman is thought of as being under the direct care of her parents, brothers and other sisters. When she is married, the sentiments involved in that care are not erased but the woman also comes under the care of her husband and his brothers.

> To meet these obligations (however unwillingly) is a matter of family honour (*Sharaf*). To fail to meet them (however willingly) is a matter of family (*a'yb*) if it is discovered by outsiders."[1]

What complicates such complex relationships are the emotionally voluptuous conflicts between a forced showing of respect, loyalty and the like and inner feelings of resentment, aloofness and disrespect. Thus, if one is put on the defensive to reveal his or her actual feelings he or she has to resort to a complex verbal expression of compliments, or *Majāmalāt*, as a means to counter constant social demands for showing affection.[2] This is true because the culture itself makes frank discussion of feelings impossible. Thus, whilst a question such as (how are you?) is viewed as a sincere gesture of inviting the other to elucidate how one feels in Western cultures, a Palestinian may view it as a passing compliment which invites immediately an identical response in a question form.

Comparative remarks aside, it should be noted that some features which are bound with the emergence of nuclear families (or even with placing equal responsibilities on individuals residing in East Jerusalem before the Israeli law)[3], comprise comprehensive understanding between spouses prior to marriage. This, of course, entails matters such as consultation with one another about domestic and non-domestic roles, managing family affairs, discussions of marital relationships and so on.[4]

Yet, in the public eye, appearing and acting as one solid unit, despite potential residues of inner feelings of apprehension, especially during crises and catastrophes, remains a fact of life. The abundance of unexpected problems associated with family members living different lifestyles, for example, result from pressures to maintain psychosocial allegiance to the extended family, *vis a vis* the welfare of one's nuclear family.

1 Gullic, J. *op. cit.* (p.131).
2 *ibid.* (p.132).
3 Further elaboration, in Chapter 2.
4 MacIver, R. *Society: A text book of Sociology*, New York, Rinehart & Co, 1948.

Unpleasant Features of Marital Life

Assessing the nature and the extent of unhappiness in marriage with any accuracy is admittedly a difficult venture. It is possible, however, to introduce variables which would tap marital adjustment, companionship and conflicts. Some of these include: i) inadequacy as a spouse, ii) frequency of irritation and tension between spouses, iii) frequency of spending leisure time or accompanying one another and iv) decision making.

Such variables can also be introduced across different age groups for the purpose of comparative analysis and in order to speculate about the family in the future.

We should recall that the unequal power base amongst spouses stems partly from the first days of contracting the marriage when the bridegroom pays an enormous price towards finalising 'the contract', which symbolises a psychological guarantee for a full devotion towards the bride, and minimal interference by her family in the groom's relationship with their daughter.

Given this scenario, the husband's hand is immediately strengthened by the community's unwritten declaration of non-interference to secure the wife's rights.

In order to tap the kinds of problems which the spouses

Table I. *Problems Faced at the Beginning of Marriage*

Main Problems	*Frequency*	*Percentage*
1. Problems associated with other spouse (sexual, differences in age and education, etc.)	136	16
2. Other human-related factors (mother-in-law, relatives, neighbours)	162	18
3. Economic hardships	132	15
4. Change in lifestyle	45	5
5. Sickness (own or other members of the family)	5	0.5
6. Living away from parents/children (*i.e.* original home)	39	4.5
7. Israeli military occupation	4	0.5
8. Other non-human related circumstances (difficulties in work, transportation, housing etc.)	56	6.5
9. No problems	261	30
10. No answer	24	3

encountered during the early stage of marriage, the following question was introduced: 'What is the main problem which you faced at the beginning of your marital life?' This was followed by another: 'What is the main problem which you face *now* in your marital life?'

Table II. *Problems Faced During* Current *Marital Life*

Main Problems	*Frequency*	*Percentage*
1. Problems associated with other spouse (sexual, differences in age and education, etc.)	80	9
2. Other human-related factors (mother-in-law, relatives, neighbours)	95	10
3. Economic hardships	196	21
4. Change in lifestyle	35	4
5. Sickness (own or other members of the family)	29	3
6. Living away from parents/children (*i.e.* original home)	11	2
7. Israeli military occupation	5	1
8. Other non-human related circumstances (difficulties in work, transportation, housing etc.)	37	4
9. No problems	389	42
10. No answer	34	4

The responses given in the previous two tables are only aggregated answers for the purpose of possible cross-tabulations with other variables, including 'age groups'. All the same, a few specific responses which were obtained during the survey are in order. Amongst the most interesting are, 'my wife stopped obeying me as before'; 'he talks more than women – you will not see his eyes when he opens his mouth'; 'routine and boredom make me neurotic'; 'I don't like her looks at home'; 'chaos'; 'loneliness'; 'jealousy'; 'people don't leave us alone'; 'responsibility' and 'her looks are as bad as her cooking'.

A comparative analysis between Tables I and II would seem appropriate with regard to select responses.

Incompatibility in sex roles and polarisation in the decision making process, as detailed in the previous chapter, has unsurprisingly brought about a relatively high response (15%; Table I) associating marital problems with the 'other' spouse. It has been argued that most of the conflicts between spouses have been reinforced by the society, which stipulates that certain roles and decisions are masculine prerogatives; others are feminine. Such responses, in addition, suggest that spouses should have better opportunities to get acquainted before marriage and a wider degree of freedom to choose one's marriage partner. Worthy of note is that once engagement had taken place amongst a Moslem couple, it is considered as binding as a wedding contract; that is, the couple cannot break it unless by a formal divorce.

The second category of responses; namely, problems related to other human factors (*e.g.* interference by relatives, neighbours and friends suggest a continuing strength of, and certainly pressure from, traditional ties.

To illustrate, we choose an observation which was made on the influence of the mother-in-law on the conjugal relations between the son and his spouse in a Chinese village.[5] Although China and the West Bank are worlds apart, they seem to share in the finest details, as can be seen from the following intricacy:

> "She (mother-in-law) feels that she has been deserted by her son, that she has lost her greatest treasure. For this she cannot blame him because she loves him so well, yet needing someone to blame, she naturally turns to his new wife. At first, she may say that her daughter-in-law should not be so appealing to her son as to make him neglect his parents, brothers and family duties. Later she may come to believe that the young woman purposely speaks against her son and a bitter resentment may grow up in her mind."

As a follow-up to the above analysis, it should be explained why fewer people (at 10%); especially from the female sub-sample, have cited other human factors as a continuing problem in their current marital life.

A patrilocal household usually signifies that the son becomes psychologically and socially dependent on his father whilst at the same time he gradually takes on the role of providing for his parents. This certainly has a characteristic effect on the bride, in

5 Yang, M. *A Chinese Village in Taitou Shantung Province*, New York, Columbia University Press, 1945 (p.61). See also Ata, I. 'Impact of Westernisation on the Moslem Women', *op. cit.*

Table III. *Problems Faced at the Beginning of Marriage (across three age groups)*

Main Problems	*Young*		*Middle-age*		*Old*	
1. Problems associated with other spouse	57	15.0%	57	13.5%	22	19.0%
2. Other human-related factors	66	17.0%	76	18.0%	20	17.0%
3. Economic hardships	63	16.5%	92	21.5%	27	23.0%
4. Change in lifestyle	16	4.0%	26	6.0%	3	2.5%
5. Sickness	3	1.0%	2	0.5%	0	0%
6. Living away from parents/children	20	5.0%	18	4.0%	1	1.0%
7. Israeli occupation	2	0.5%	2	0.5%	0	0%
8. Other non-human related circumstances	25	6.5%	26	6.0%	5	4.0%
9. No problems	117	30.5%	109	25.5%	35	30.0%
10. No answer	9	2.3%	12	3.0%	3	2.5%

Table IV. *Problems Faced During* Current *Marital Life (across three age groups)*

Main Problems	Young		Middle-age		Old	
1. Problems associated with other spouse	32	8.5%	39	9.0%	9	8.0%
2. Other human-related factors (problems/obligations imposed from outside)	41	10.0%	50	11.0%	4	3.5%
3. Economic hardships	63	16.5%	104	24.5%	29	25.0%
4. Change in lifestyle	15	4.0%	14	3.0%	6	5.0%
5. Sickness	7	2.0%	12	3.0%	10	8.0%
6. Living away from parents/children	4	1.0%	5	1.0%	2	1.5%
7. Israeli occupation	2	0.5%	3	0.5%	0	0%
8. Other non-human related circumstances	25	6.5%	12	3.0%	0	0%
9. No problems	175	45.5%	164	38.5%	50	43.0%
10. No answer	14	3.5%	16	4.0%	4	3.5%

that she becomes subordinate to her mother-in-law (who maintains some degree of control over the household). In time, however, the wife's status and power increase within the household as her children become grown-up. In a later section, it will become clearer how and why the majority of the sample cited 'having children' as the most pleasing feature of their marital life. (Table V in the Appendix).

Before proceeding with the analysis it would be relevant to include results of the three age groups in the following two tables. Sufficient to note that the differences amongst the three age groups for most response categories are very slight.

Proceeding with analysis, one registers a sizeable 20% and 21% (Tables I and II, respectively) citing 'economic hardships' as an intervening (problematic) factor in their marital life. A comprehensive analysis of this subject is found in an earlier chapter. It would be of relevance, however, to note that families who have occupied their house for decades will continue to do so because of economic necessity. The Jordanian law, which is still enacted in the whole of the West Bank except for East Jerusalem, does not permit the landowner to raise his rent so long as the same tenant is occupying the residence. The tenant will have to contend himself with any basic irreparable fault because of the relatively inexpensive rent.

Responses indicating that there are no problems at all draw a large percentage in all four tables. Such responses are exacerbated by the reality that (Islamic) religion and society do not allow frank expression of one's inner feelings. The emotional suppression of one's feelings usually leads to pretenses that they do not exist.[6] The psychological after-effects of such a repressive process need a psychoanalytic explanation.

Living away from parents (*i.e.* from one's original home) was a response that registered a noticeable 4%, in Table I. A tendency on the bride's part to complain about living away from home results from the psychological and mental surprise at being removed into a stranger's house, and subsequently losing her father's protection. Further, an increased migratory trend by young males, running away from conditions of hardship, added to the parents' unenviable state of affairs.

6 Khatchadorian, H. 'The mask and the face: a study of make believe in Middle Eastern society' in *Middle East Forum*, Vol. 37, 1961 (pp.15–18).

Dynamic State of Marital Relationships

A clear description of the dynamics of interaction between spouses is almost a non-event because of the intricate subtleties involved.

One thing remains clear however; that men's preference to seclude themselves from women, especially at times of social visits, playing backgammon in small cafés, or gathering in somebody's shop, invites different levels of analysis.

For starters, maintaining separate worlds between men and women, public and private, helps to secure the honour and chastity concept,[7] by guaranteeing that no mixing shall take place between the sexes. The segregation of the sexes would seem to be partly in order to prevent extra or pre-marital affairs, or at least to make them much more difficult.

Unlike their sexual counterparts, men in a sexually isolated environment often find it opportune to extol their domination and authority by gossiping about it to whoever happens to be around.

This, of course, is perpetuated by a widespread belief in the society that men do not belong at home, that only women do, and therefore that men can spend most of their time outside it. If, however, the man spends most of his time at home he will not draw sufficient respect from others; namely, from other men who would consider him somewhat feminine and sissy. He would thus be described *Muchanath*; that is, someone who mixes with women and displays 'unmanly' characteristics.

As regards women, their main duty has been socialising and care of children. This role has been exaggerated as a result of the husband's long absence from home, and the male's minimal communication with females. Rarely did the household head (the husband) interfere with domestic tasks, including moral upbringing of his children. Instead, his overall concern was managing single-handedly the daily and future affairs of the family. This was primarily prompted by their highly regarded social status, and ill-consideration of the wife's rather sensitive and adequate participation in such tasks.

The indoor–outdoor behaviour stemmed from dividing space into a man's world and a woman's world. The former is the world where men are given the right of outdoor free movement and

[7] Refer to appropriate thesis, 'Honour, compared to 1967, etc' (pp.159–160).

pursuing individual entertainment in other circumstances. The incessant activity and employment of working and cooking utensils by women through week-days, give men an additional incentive to seek temporary refuge outside the home.

Free-time does occur, but it is usually utilised in the same tense, infested residence by the wife's visiting or inviting female neighbours to exchange various local news on the affairs of other families, listening to music as they handle shell-cased nuts.

Mernissi finds that in the patriarchal household, as the case is on the West Bank, what amounts to a theme of 'almost conscious determined repression of the husband–wife relationship'.[8] An example of the absence of public display of interest by either spouse was uttered during one of the interviews:

> "He (the husband) went to buy a scarf for me, but decided to buy three instead. His mother had to make first choice both for her and her daughters. I had to choose the one left behind."

In order to gauge how much of a companion husbands view their wives; that is, how much are family relationships allowed to have a place in society in the modern Western sense, the following question was introduced: 'How often do you accompany your spouse when you go out?'

Illustrated in Table V are the various responses to this question.[9]

Table V. *Frequency of Spouses Accompanying One Another (across three age groups)*

	All the time		*Most times*		*Occasionally*		*Never*	
1. Young	41	10.5%	83	21.5%	201	52.5%	58	15.0%
2. Middle-age	40	9.5%	95	22.0%	203	47.5%	88	20.5%
3. Old	12	10.0%	28	24.0%	58	50.0%	18	15.5%
	93	10.0%	206	22.5%	462	50.0%	164	17.5%

Kendall's Tau $C = 0.014$; Significance $= 0.29$
Gamma $= 0.024$

[8] Mernissi, F. *Beyond the Veil: Male–Female Dynamics in a Modern Moslem Society*. New York, John Wiley & Sons, 1975 (pp.76–77).

[9] Separate tables for male and female sub-samples can be found in the Appendix.

Results taken from the Kendall's Tau *C* test indicates a casual relationship (at 0.024) between the two variables: age, and the tendency of accompanying one's spouse. The percentage of those who indicated that they occasionally take their spouses out with them is very large (50%). Another 17.5% indicated that they do not take their spouses out with them at all.

Further, the analysis of variance in the *t*-test was employed for the purpose of comparative analysis between the different groups (Table VI). The results obtained clearly show the differences in the mean responses between the 'Young' the 'Middle-aged' and the 'Old' to be insignificant; that is, the null hypothesis must be accepted.

Table VI. *(*t*-test results) of Frequency of Spouses Accompanying One Another (across three age groups)*

	All/most of the time	*Occasionally*	*Total*
1. Young	123	201	324
2. Middle-age	136	203	339
3. Old	40	58	98
	299	462	761

$f = 5.02$; $f < F\ (0.95, 2, 3) = 9.55$; $5.02 < 9.55$
Accept H_0

It would seem reasonable to note that the absence of Western-style restaurants, coffee places and modern theatres in the West Bank is a certain assurance of a good female behaviour outside the house. Two kinds of institution seem to have, in a relative sense, evaded this restriction: the universities (and some community colleges) and some clubs which are associated with Christian churches and missionaries, where opportunities of mixing is nearly a natural happening.[10]

Given that the majority of the sample never or rarely accompany their spouses when they go out, the opportunities of having contact in public, become scarcer. This should partly explain why fewer people (238) indicated that they have scolded their spouses

[10] A comparative study between group affiliations of Christian and Moslem communities on this subject area is forthcoming.

in public than those who did not (667); (Table VII). Results in the *t*-test rule out any significant differences in the mean responses amongst the different age groups.

Table VII. *Frequency of Spouses Scolding Their Counterparts in Public (Q: 'Have you scolded your spouse in public during the last month?')*

	Yes	*No*	*Total*
1. Young	107	273	380
2. Middle-age	102	313	415
3. Old	29	81	110
	238	667	905

$f = 1.1$; $f < F\ (0.95, 2, 3) = 9.55$; $1.1 < 9.55$
Accept H_0

Table VIII. *Frequency of Spouses Being Scolded by Their Counterparts in Public (Q: 'Have you been scolded by your counterpart in public during the last month?')*

	Yes	*No*	*Total*
1. Young	103	279	382
2. Middle-age	112	313	425
3. Old	34	81	115
	249	673	922

$f = 1.14$; $f < F\ (0.95, 2, 3) = 9.55$; $1.14 < 9.55$
Accept H_0

Yet, in spite of the above categorisation of the results, a sizeable percentage (57%; Table IX) indicated that they prefer to have a discussion with their spouses whenever there was a difference of opinion about a common issue of concern. The responses to this category, however, are not equally distributed among the three age groups. Of the 'Young' group 66.8% indicated that they would have a discussion in times of disagreements, 30.7% of the 'Middle-age' group gave a similar response, and only 47.4% of the 'Older' group indicated the same.

The direction of the results is reversed for those who indicated that they would completely concede their opinions if they sense a potentially negative effect on their marital life. These responses were distributed as follows: 'young' group – 18%; 'middle-age' – 29.6%; 'old' group – 31%.

Like any other place, problems in marriage on the West Bank indicate an absence in family arbitration, and can be viewed as disuniting grounds, leading to unsettled disputes. There certainly is, however, a brighter side to marriage. This is discussed in the following section.

Pleasant Features in Marital Life

Introduction

It has already been noted that family structure on the West Bank is a replica of any patrilineal household; that is, one in which the extended family results from the father and his male descendants who reside patrilocally after marriage.[11] It follows that by linking past, present and future generations through patrilineal inheritance, the relationship between husband and wife becomes influenced by the corporate character of the family.

The outcome of this kind of relationship is one whereby marriage becomes organised more from the standpoint of cohesion of the family than by personal choice. Indeed, its significance as a social unit surpasses its biological significance.

Accordingly, we find firstly that many families arranged marriages and, secondly, that the primary purpose of marrying tends to be the production of heirs. In fact, production of children becomes an issue that is more over-riding than (and ultimately precludes) any intimate communication and emotional satisfaction. Love relationship and mutual attraction between the spouses are not of primary importance, and subsequently are no longer the basis of marital arrangements. Sometimes there are expressed romances, but they often have nothing to do with marriage. Certainly, economic considerations are regarded as 'practical' considerations, but it has little to do with 'love'.

Fulfilling one's aspirations of bearing children soon after marriage is the most highly prized possession, not only for women but for the rest of the extended family, not to mention distant

[11] Michaelson, E. and Goldschmidt, W. *op. cit.* (1971).

relations, neighbours and friends. An Arab sociologist elaborates:

> "The fear of being a 'barren' woman is not eliminated until the first pregnancy has occurred. From month to month after marriage, the new bride hopes and prays that she does not menstruate, for she has been told that missing the menstrual period is a sign of pregnancy. The eagerness of the bride's parents, husband and in-laws for this sign is not any less than that of the bride herself, for all of them are anxious to see that the bride is not barren."[12]

It can thus be inferred how restless members of the family remain until signs of fertility are witnessed or announced. Only if the wife is declared able to bear children will others become relaxed and proud that the family lineage and socio-economic well-being is secured. The benefits which parents derive as a result vary from purely monetary to non-monetary factors.

In order to verify our hypotheses, we introduced the following question to the sample: 'What is the most pleasant feature in your marital life?'

Table X outlines the given responses, of which 'my children' elicited the second largest response (29.3%). Noteworthy is that the responses of the male and female sub-samples can be found separately classified in the Appendix. Certainly, detailed responses have been aggregated into broader classification for the purpose of effective cross-tabulations.

One needs to keep in mind that the birth of the first child never quenches the parents' desire to have one or more children. In so doing, they have secured themselves against any misfortunes which the first-born might encounter. In addition, they have another chance should the first-born happen to be a daughter. The value of having a son(s) rests with the fact that 'he can carry the name of the family and take care of us when we age' (interview 301).

With regards to having daughters, though they may not give their parents prestige in the eyes of the society, their importance in helping with the work of the house is well-recognised. Said a mother with two teenage daughters: 'When I went to my sister's

[12] Gadalla, S. 'The influence of reproduction norms on family size and fertility behaviour!' in S. E. Ibrahim *ed. op. cit.* (p.328); see also MacIver, R. *op. cit.* (p.20).

Table IX. *Responses to the Question: 'What would you do if you had a difference of opinion with your wife?' (three age groups)*

	'Would keep opinion even if it affects my marriage'		*'Would concede if it affects my marriage'*		*'Would discuss differences'*		*Non-revelant responses*		*No answer*	
1. Young	32	8.5%	69	18.0%	256	66.8%	23	6.0%	3	1.0%
2. Middle-age	56	13.0%	126	29.6%	216	50.7%	24	5.6%	4	1.0%
3. Old	13	11.2%	36	31.0%	55	47.4%	11	9.5%	1	1.0%
		10.9%		25.0%		57.0%		6.3%		9.0%

Table X. *Pleasing Features about Marital Life*

Features	*Frequency*	*Percentage*
1. Understanding Spouse	370	40.0
2. Children	271	29.3
3. Having sex	6	0.6
4. Having responsibility	141	15.2
5. Being settled	21	2.3
6. Freedom, entertainment	2	0.2
7. Other peripheral responses (*e.g.* cooking)	8	0.9
8. Everything	47	5.1
9. Nothing	48	5.2
10. No answer	11	1.2
	925	100.0

funeral in Amman, all the cooking, washing, and taking care of Abu-Issa (the father) was just as good as if I had done it by myself' (interview 111).

Inability to have children, particularly male children, is usually sufficient reason to disrupt marital relationships, since a great portion of the husband's honour is embodied in his virility. It is common belief that:

> "Men's virility is proved by having a large offspring, especially males, since male children are able to assure the perpetuity of the lineage."[13]

Attitudes between Palestinians/Arabs and Westerners towards having children is quite distinct. The Western family refrains from having children if it cannot afford to do so; this being a function of having a feeling of responsibility towards the unborn, coupled with their unwillingness to bring children into the world unless they can guarantee a security of their well-being. This feeling of anxiety is not present in almost all Arab cultures, since children are (inadvertently) a promising form of investment in the absence of some form of social security. To a Westerner, it is astonishing to learn that a few older sons do not even marry so that they can guarantee

[13] Escribano, M. *op. cit.* (p.11); see also Karan, M. 'Une fois un Arab une fois des Arabes . . .' *Les Temps Modernes*, Sept.–Oct. 1972 (p.347).

a good upbringing and a reasonable level of education of their younger siblings.

The duty of maintaining the family has been entrusted by the *Sharia*, the religious Islamic law, to the man; the bringing up of children to the woman.[14] Cultural proverbs abound with blessings for couples who perform the good deed. Examples which are heard almost on a daily basis are: *El-Walad Bihid Balad* ('a son can ruin a whole town'); *El-Walad Sanad* ('the son is like a crutch'); and, 'there is nothing more precious than the son except the son's son'; 'a house is like a paradise, without sons it is not at all beautiful'; 'Allah protects him until he becomes as tall as a minaret'; and, *Ajaham Fahed wu bifleh* ('they brought a stud and he produces also').

Because the birth of a son is so valued, through it the mother subsequently enjoys more respect, protection and guarantees. For example, if the son graduates in medicine, the mother's title changes from *Sitt* (Mrs . . .) into *Imm Edduktōr* (the doctor's mother). Clearly then, most of her emotional ties and psychological well-being centre on her relationship with her son.

The feeling is also true with having daughters, especially as they are guaranteed a bride price – though consciously this is not said in so many words.

Data regarding the family's perception that there is no harm in having more children than originally planned is not presented in this study. Without any doubt the overwhelming majority would express positive feelings about exceeding the number of children that they planned for.[15]

With respect to results obtained from the Chi-square test, differences between the three age groups proved significant, and

[14] Lichtenstadter, I. *Women in the Aiyam al-Arab*, London, The Royal Asiatic Society, 1935 (p.81).

[15] In his book *Al Tagheer Al Ijtimaī wa al-TawaFuq al-Nafsi* (Social Changes and Psychological Congruence), 1978 (p.79) Kamana cites that the mean average of children which a Palestinian woman has in her lifetime is 7.4. Although accurate figures *re* West Bank Palestinians are difficult to secure, the mean average of children is presumed to be a little lower. In another study of the demography of Amman, the average size of a Christian household was 5.6 persons, as opposed to 7 persons in a Moslem household (see Hacker, J. *Modern Amman: A Social Study*) Research Paper Series No. 3, Durham, Durham Colleges, 1960 (p.75).

the null hypothesis is subsequently rejected (Table XI). In specific terms, the proportion of the 'Old' age-group, indicating children as being the most pleasant feature in marital life, is statistically larger than both the 'Middle-age' group and the 'Young' group. It would seem correct to ascertain that the younger the age group the less is the tendency to cite children as the most pleasant feature. The young age-group may be placing more emphasis on matters which are intertwined with the nature and viability of the husband–wife relationship. It is also possible that in bilateral family structures – *vis a vis* patrilineal descent – there is less emphasis on producing male children, and less reserve between the spouses.

Table XI. *χ^2-test of Responses Indicating 'Children' as the Most Pleasant Feature in Marital Life (controlling for three age groups)*

	Frequency O_{ij}	E_{ij}	Total responses
1. Young	103	112	382
2. Middle-age	128	100	426
3. Old	40	34	116
	271	246	924

$\chi^2 = 9.56$
$\chi^2\ (0.995; 1) = 7.879$
$\chi^2 > \chi^2\ (0.995; 1)$. Reject H_0

Table XII. *Responses indicating 'children' as the most pleasant feature in marital life; controlling for Area*

Area	Frequency	Percentage	Total responses (frequency)
Cities			
1. Hebron	52	26.0	200
2. Jerusalem	62	31.5	197
Villages			
3. Jiffna	50	37.3	134
4. Khader	18	12.3	146
Camps			
5. Dhaisha	26	25.0	104
6. Tul-Karem	63	43.8	144

Likewise, it was anticipated that the same reasoning would apply to village dwellers, *i.e.*, Khader and Jiffna. However, the results obtained in Table XII were inconsistent with this hypothesis.

The highest category of response was that which indicated that 'communicating with' and 'understanding spouse' was the most pleasant feature in one's marital life. Out of a total 924 subjects, 371 gave the above responses. However, there were no significant responses between the three age groups in the Chi-square test (Table XIII).

Table XIII. *χ^2 test of Responses Indicating 'Understanding Spouse' as the Most Pleasant Feature in Marital Life (controlling for three age groups)*

	Frequency		
	O_{ij}	E_{ij}	*Total responses*
1. Young	171	153.38	382
2. Middle-age	165	171.05	426
3. Old	35	46.60	116
	371	371.03	924

$\chi^2 = 5.13$
$\chi^2\ (0.995; 1) = 7.879$
$\chi^2 > \chi^2\ (0.995; 1)$. Accept H_0

Citing 'having responsibility' triggered a relatively smaller response; yet like the previous table, no significant differences were found between the three age groups in the Chi-square test (Table XIV).

Despite the large number of subjects indicating a variety of so-called 'pleasant' responses about their marital life, a few indicated that there are a number of aspects about their pre-marital life which they miss (Table XV). Results obtained in Kendall's Tau *C* test show that there is a significant relationship between the two variables being part of a certain age group and the tendency of giving a certain kind of response.

The direction of the results in Table XV support the assumption that the older the age group is the higher the proportion of those who do not miss anything about their pre-marital life becomes. Of the 'Old' group 44% miss their pre-marital life and a higher

Table XIV. *χ^2-test of Responses Indicating 'Having Responsibility' as the Most Pleasant Feature in Marital Life (controlling for three age groups)*

	O_{ij}	E_{ij}	*Total responses*
1. Young	43	52.58	382
2. Middle-age	47	47.5	426
3. Old	13	12.9	116
	103	112.98	924

$\chi^2 = 0.01$
χ^2 (0.995; 1) = 7.879
$\chi^2 < \chi^2$ (0.995; 1), Accept H_0

percentage (55.2%) do not; of the 'Middle-age' group 50.2% indicated that they do and 49.1% indicated otherwise; whilst a higher proportion of the 'Young' age group (57.7%) miss it, and 41.5% do not. As regards differences in the response results obtained in the *t*-test show that they are significant, but only between the 'Middle-age' and the 'Old' groups. At the 6.00 level of significance, the null hypothesis was thus rejected.

It would stand to reason to conclude that, either the young generation is having more illusions about marriage and are being frank about their responses, or sex roles are becoming less polarised, and thus more conscious strategies for dealing with emerging role strains are required. Clearly this needs to be

Table XV. *Responses to the Question: 'Do you miss any premarital aspects of your life?' (across three age groups)*

		Yes		*No*	*Missing value*
(M1) 1. Young	221	57.5%	159	41.5%	
(M2) 2. Middle-age	214	50.2%	209	49.1%	
(M3) 3. Old	51	44.0%	64	55.2%	
		52.5%		46.7%	8%

Chi-square = 8.529; 4 degrees freedom; Significance = 0.07
Kendall's Tau C = 0.074; Significance = .002
Missing Value = 7
t = 6.0; t (0.995, 3) = 5.841
t>5.841 = t (0.995, 3); Reject H_0 (M2 and M3)

examined in a totally independent study. Suffice to observe Goode's[16] remark that any changes do bring with them a certain degree of frustration. But these changes are welcome, because they bring with them a wide range and freedom of choice, and an increase in the availability of options.

Results obtained in Table XVI stand against any possibilities of statistical differences in the responses between the three age groups, regarding the very aspects which they miss in 'their pre-marital life'. The two largest responses for the three age groups (combined) are categorised at 19.4% who miss entertainment, hobbies and rest; 20.0% miss 'freedom'; and 6.5% miss being close to relatives and other family members.

Marriage Conditions Pre and Post 1967

In order to find out whether marital conditions on the West Bank were better or worse before 1967, for whatever reason, we introduced a question to that effect. The results emerged as indicated in Table XVII. The sample is almost equally divided between 399 who thought that marriage conditions were actually better after 1967, and about 397 who thought otherwise.

Employing an 'Analysis of variance' in the *t*-test, no significant differences were noted amongst the response ratios of the three age groups.

Table XVII. *Comparative Responses* re *Marriage Conditions Pre and Post 1967 (across three age groups)*

	Better after 1967	*Worse after 1967*	*Total*
1. Young	213	117	330
2. Middle-age	158	211	369
3. Old	28	70	98
	399	398	797

$f = 4.67$; $f<F$ (0.95, 2, 3) = 9.95; 4.67<9.55
Accept H_0
(In addition, another 114 indicated 'the same', as their response)

The reasons identified behind the responses in the previous table was quite varied, and somewhat enlightening as they appear in Table XVIII.

[16] *op. cit.*

Table XVI. *Aspects of Pre-marital life being missed by sample*

	Entertainment hobbies, rest, furthering education		*Being close to parents/ family*		*Freedom*		*Going back to Palestine*		*Lack of responsibility*		*Don't know*		*No answer*	
	Freq.	*Percen.*	*Freq.*	*Percen.*	*Freq.*	*Percen.*	*Freq.*	*Percen.*	*Freq.*	*Percen.*	*Freq.*	*Percen.*	*Freq.*	*Percen.*
1. Young	79	20.6	17	23.5	90	23.5	7	1.8	28	7.3	1	0.3	161	42.0
2. Middle-age	78	18.3	34	8.0	80	18.8	5	1.2	17	4.0	0	0.0	211	49.0
3. Old	22	19.0	9	7.8	15	12.9	3	2.6	4	3.4	0	0.0	63	54.0
Total	177	19.4	60	6.5	185	20.0	15	1.6	49	5.3	1	1.0	435	47.0

Table XVIII. *Reasons Behind Comparative Responses in Marriage Conditions Pre and Post 1967*

	Frequency	*Percentage*		*Frequency*	*Percentage*
1. Inflation – economic hardship	141	15.2	11. Freedom in choosing spouse	147	15.9
2. Political conditions	60	6.5	12. Loss of Palestine	2	0.2
3. Division of labour between sexes	5	0.5	13. Marriage is based on love (worse now)	3	0.3
4. Bride paid expenses	43	4.6	14. The individual is becoming his own master	9	1.0
5. Increase of problems/demands	45	4.9	15. Accommodation	9	1.0
6. Increase of individual freedom	54	5.8	16. No change at all	59	6.4
7. Change of ethical values	67	7.2	17. Understanding between spouses	67	7.2
8. Change in socio-economic conditions	99	10.7	18. Maturity in marital relationships	25	2.7
9. Absence of reservation by female	8	0.9	19. Curbing of freedom	2	0.2
10. Equality in sex roles and social status	17	1.8	20. No answer	65	0.7

Chapter VIII

Summary and Conclusions

This study has been concerned with aspects of change in marital relationships which the West Bank Palestinian family have undergone during three generations of its evolution.

The study was based on a survey sample of 925 randomly selected households serving as a basis for analysis. The survey sample was sorted out from three primary milieux reflecting variations in Palestinian life; namely, city inhabitants, town dwellers and camp refugees. The two cities were (Arab) East Jerusalem and Hebron, the villages were those of Jiffna and Khader and the two refugee camps were Dhaisha and Tul-Karem.

The six areas were selected because of the geographical, religious, conservative/liberal population distribution, variation in lifestyle and, in order to make possible controlling the slightest irregularities and consistencies that are displayed by the three age groups. For example, East Jerusalem is of a unique interest not only because it is the most ethnically and religiously diverse urban centre, but because it was forcibly annexed to Israel and is being transformed in its demographic, social, cultural, historical, and physical features. Subsequently, comparative observations between the family in Jerusalem and that in the West Bank are made in the hope that they will pròvide more insight to the conclusions that are reached.

The study presented the reader with the first comprehensive study of the evolution of the character of the Palestinian family on the West Bank of Jordan.

Primarily, the study focused on the following areas:

a) Marital decision making, division of labour, family role

enactment and aspirations for the future.
b) The salient features were compatability in relationships and adjustment to marital life.
c) Family changes which accompany ageing and the way they manifest themselves amongst town, village and camp inhabitants and to a lesser degree between spouses.

Statistical testing has primarily served our research process in separating significant results, and in determining the acceptability of hypotheses and the assumptions which underlie each of them. Though the results obtained are open to challenge and criticism because of the crudeness and unreliability of some of the indicators used for measurement, their very crudeness speaks well for the substance of the research for, even as crude measures with reliability in some cases, they do work as they were intended to.

It should be observed that an increasing correlation of variables in the opposite direction is still valid, if examined, refined and corrected. Despite the poor statistical results obtained, attention may be drawn to the extent to which such alterations may affect the theory described above.

With respect to the background characteristics of households under focus, it was observed that such factors provided explanations of many of the results. Likewise, the effects of the occupation on the community should not be ignored. Detailed in this study, for example, are the many strains which the invasion of highly-inflated Israeli products placed on the very entity of the Palestinian family.

The prevailing characteristics of the sample are noted below:
a) There are 452 wives and 473 husbands (from different households) distributed as follows – 200 in Hebron, 197 in East Jerusalem, 134 in Jiffna, 146 in Khader, 104 in Dhaisha and 144 in Tul-Karem.
b) The three age groups (generations) are divided into 'Young' – lower than 33 years of age, 'Middle-age' – 34–53 years and 'Old' – 54 years and over.
c) Of the female sub-sample, 81.8% are housewives, though the female ratio in the professional category (8.5%) is very close to that of the male sub-sample (11.3%).

There are marked differences, however, amongst the three age groups in the 'housewife' and 'unemployed' categories. Of the 'Old' age sub-sample, 31% are housewives and 10.3% are unemployed, compared with 43.3% and 1.3% respectively, in the 'Young' age sub-sample. The unskilled 'Young' and 'Middle-age' sub-samples total 24.3% and 23% respectively; whereas, the unskilled 'Old' sub-sample totals 37.9%. The latter group has also a relatively high figure of unemployed individuals reaching 10.3%; as opposed to a respective 1.3% and 1.6% in the 'Young' and 'Middle-age' categories.

Obstacles to economic growth on the West Bank after 1967 are analysed and its effect on the Palestinian family is clearly noted. It should be noted however that the effects of wage-labour opportunities contributed towards narrowing the social status cleavages, originally instigated by variations of family ownership of land, as well as marginalisation of land.

d) The results obtained clearly attest to changes towards an improvement in education amongst the 'Young' generation for both males and females. Tables XII and XIII (Chapter IV) show, for example, that there are three times as many 'Young' who have completed or partly-completed secondary schooling as 'Old' people have. The gap goes wider still regarding completing a diploma of higher education.

The trends in Table XIV (Chapter IV) show that camp refugees reflect the highest proportion of illiteracy (Dhaisha, 21.2%; Tul-Karem, 34.0%), followed by villagers (Jiffna, 9.0%; Khader, 21.2%). The numbers are much lower for city dwellers (Hebron, 4.5%; Jerusalem, 5.1%). At the other end of the scale, city dwellers reflect the highest level of tertiary education with Jerusalem instituting 13.0% and Hebron 11.2% of their total samples. The ratio of tertiary educated village inhabitants constitutes 3.7% of the Jiffna sample, and 3.4% for Khader. The ratio of tertiary-educated people from Dhaisha refugee camp stands at 4.8% and from Tul-Karem camp at 0.7%.

e) Tables XV and XVI show that the mean age at marriage for the Palestinian male is 23.6 years and the female average is 19.6. The youngest males in the sample married at the age of 14. Comparatively, females who indicated that their age at marriage was between 12–15 years were 75 in number, or 16.7% of the total female sub-sample.

f) The mean number of children per family was estimated at 4.9. It is interesting, however, to point out that no significant differences were detected in the mean of the number of children between urban and rural families.

g) Attempts at introducing religious affiliation as a variable were postponed for a future study. Suffice to observe that of those asked about their religion not a single respondent abstained from identifying with the religion of his ancestry. The results were divided between 714 (or 77%) Moslems; 209 Christians (or 23% of the sample). The two 'missing values' were the result of a statistical error.

As regards the concepts of honour, chastity and social organisations in a following section, they were observed to be clearly interconnected. Blood marriages, for example, were cited as the preferred kind for many reasons. Firstly, they are said to make for smoother relations in the household, to maintain and strengthen existing ties and cohesion among its members and to preserve and arrange property within the kinship group.

Not surprisingly, a total of 42% of the sample indicated that they have blood relationship with their spouse, 57% indicated otherwise and 8 cases were considered missing values.

Significant differences were discovered between the 'Young' and 'Old' sub-samples in the mean responses of having 'blood relationship' with their spouses. A high level of 45.7% of the 'Old' age group indicated having blood relationship prior to marriage and 53.4% did not, whereas 41.1% of the 'Young' age group indicated having a blood relationship with 57.4% indicating that they did not.

The 'statistical' decrease in endogamous marriages can be partly explained because of the continuous migration of young males to more stable, economically and politically secure countries. It is equally true that a large number of Palestinian males who go to study in Western countries end up marrying there, away from their close family.

It was also found that with respect to blood marriages amongst village and camp sub-samples, the proportion of relatives marrying was relatively higher than that in the cities.

The fact that a fair number of marriages are pre-arranged was clearly shown in the overall responses. Almost one third of the female sub-sample indicated that their husbands 'chose' them – an admission reflecting their acceptance of the practice of being passive in the whole affair. Interestingly, however, as many as 33 wives (7.0%) indicated that they chose their husbands; as opposed to 3 husbands or (0.7%) who gave this kind of response.

Of the male sub-sample, 39% indicated that their family chose their wives, as opposed to 32.6% of the female sub-sample who gave the same response, *i.e.* that their husband's family had chosen them.

A cursory glance at the results in Table V (Chapter 5) suggests an association in the relationship (at the 0.009 level; Kendall's Tau test) between the age of the female sub-sample and the responses as to who selected them for marriage. As the sample 'becomes younger' the tendency of future male spouses to have a final say in selecting their counterparts increases; whilst the tendency of the family of the male (and indeed the female) to select his wife for him decreases.

Results obtained in Table VI (Chapter 5) also show that, at the 0.01 level of significance, there is an association in the relationship between the age of the male sub-sample and the responses as to who selected their wives for marriage. In the category of the 'Young', for example, the ratio of those who indicated that they themselves had chosen their wives was twice as high (at 112 responses) as that of those who indicated that their family had (at 61 responses). It is not surprising to note that the number of those who indicated their wives' family as the main selectors were much lower than those in the female sub-sample.

The rationale given by those who expressed that interracial marriages are 'good', but only between Palestinian females and 'Western' males was clear. Palestinian females were more likely to be faithful to their Western spouses than Western females to Palestinian husbands.

Free mixing of young Palestinian men and women, especially in public places, is still largely foreign to the Palestinian West Bank culture. Subsequently, it is not strange to learn that women who did not have prior acquaintance with men accept whatever sentiments they felt towards their menfolk as love.

Suspecting, that the male sub-sample would, for obvious reasons, give biased responses to the question; 'had you ever spoken to your wife before marriage?' they were spared the opportunity. Results regarding the female sub-sample show that they were unproportionally divided between a sizeable 58% indicating that they never spoke to their husbands prior to marriage, and 40% indicating otherwise (Table VII, Chapter 5).

The direction of the relationship between the two responses among the three age groups is consistent with our hypothesis; that is, that there is an association in the relationship between the two variables 'age' and 'premarital speech' (at the 0.0004 level). It is apparent that the younger sub-sample displays a greater tendency to have verbal encounters with their wives-to-be than the 'Middle-age' or the 'Old' generations. It would seem right to assume that the 'Young' generation is venturing gradually, particularly in the four universities, to meeting privately, and certainly talking, with one another before marriage.

This, of course, is a slight detour from tradition, where the norm is for the man to mix and socialise more frequently with female members of his ancestral family, including his mother, whose financial dependence on her son is her raison d'être.

Six variables are introduced in Chapter VI in order to tap any possible differences in the authority structure and decision making processes between the two sexes and across the three age groups. These are, a) provision of income, b) care of children, c) cleaning of house, d) discipline of children, e) family entertainment and f) visits with relatives and friends.

With regards to all the six indices employed, no consistent differences in the responses were noted amongst the three age groups. The income was predominantly the responsibility of the male. Conversely, the majority of the three age groups uniformly indicated that 'care of children' and 'house cleaning' were two domestic roles for which the wife is solely responsible.

Regarding the last three measures, two thirds indicated that 'both' spouses are responsible for 'disciplining children' and 'family entertainment', compared with one third indicating the wife for the former role and one third indicating the husband for the latter role. Regarding family contact and visits, two thirds indicated that this role should be jointly enacted and one third indicated that it should be the husband's responsibility.

Results obtained as to who was the primary force behind the present distribution of duties and roles show that the mean responses across the three age groups, are uniform; reflecting no statistical difference except for family entertainment (Table XXVIII, Chapter 6). It is indicated that the proportion of those who took a joint decision amongst the 'Old' group towards entertainment of the family was greater than the proportion of families in which the husband took the decision alone; this being the opposite response to that in the 'Middle-age' families.

It is clear, then, that the Palestinian family is basically male-dominated and patriarchal. Women, it was found, do have a certain impact in the family's decision, but only in as far as 'traditional' female-oriented duties are concerned.

Yet, the most interesting results obtained are those in response to a 'preferred' role, given appropriate circumstances and an *ideal* society. Though none of the differences in the mean responses across the three age groups are significant, the overall direction of the responses has changed. Specifically, the proportion of those preferring a 'shared responsibility' in domestic and non-domestic roles across the three age groups has more than doubled, according to certain measures.

The overall changes between the present roles and the 'preferred' future roles regarding the six indicators are statistically significant in the Chi-square test. This means that the authority structure has been maintained by choice, circumstances, pressure, or a combination of both. The gap between the three age groups seems evident, despite the continuing strength of traditional ties. Nevertheless it is the consensus of the majority on the measured indices that in *ideal* circumstances, traditional values regarding sex roles and division of labour should be altered in favour of women.

And, finally we asked what are the dynamics of interrelationships between the spouses and across the three age groups.

Incompatibility in sex roles and decision making has, not surprisingly, brought about a relatively high response (15%; Table I, Chapter 7) associating problems with the 'other spouse'. The second category of responses, namely problems related to 'other human factors', such as interferences by relatives, neighbours and friends, suggests a continuing strength and certainly pressure of traditional ties. Another sizeable number (20%; Table I, Chapter 7) cited economic hardships as intervening problematic factors in their marital life.

The perceived differences amongst the three age groups on all responses of this measure are very slight.

Results taken from Kendall's Tau *C* test (Table V, Chapter 7) indicate a casual relationship (at the 0.02 level) between the two variables: age and the tendency of accompanying one's spouse when one goes out. 50% of the sample indicated that they occasionally take their spouses out with them, another 17.5% do not at all. Differences in the mean responses between the three age groups are significant on this measure.

In response to 'what is the most pleasant feature in your marital life?', the second bulk of responses comprised the statement, 'my children'. It was noted that the proportion of the 'Old' age group who cited this response is significantly larger than both the 'Middle-age' and the 'Young' groups. It would seem correct to ascertain that the younger the age group, the lesser the tendency to cite 'children' as the most pleasant feature in one's life. Instead, the 'Young' age group, it is assumed, may be placing more emphasis on matters which are intertwined with the nature and viability of the husband–wife relationship. It is also speculated that in bilateral family structures – *vis a vis* patrilineal descent – there is less emphasis on producing male children and less reserve between the spouses.

And, finally, the preceding data and discussions show that certain changes in the family structure in the West Bank are taking place across the three age groups. Yet, in a number of other areas of behaviour, *e.g.* decision making and sex roles, tradition continues to prevail. To what extent has the Israeli 'intervening' variables perpetuated polarised feelings and attitudes between parents and children is a subject to be probed further. Evidently, the more exposure to the Israeli culture is hardly an adequate explanation for the changes that continue to occur with the family.

Another area that warrants further study is, whether as a result of the occupation, a feeling that an improvement in the status of women is both necessary and compatible with cultural values. It is speculated that by granting more freedom of choice to women, not only will it make them enter into more spheres of national life and become more productive, but that their effect on socialising the younger generation will be a contributing factor to the national norm.

Certainly, as men and women become more liberated (having more imagination for a better and more tasteful life) in the face of restraining forces within the society the moral basis for behaviour loses its consideration. The image of the society becomes thus vague and diffused, and gives rise to conflicts of loyalty and deteriorating cohesion among different sections of the community. Inevitably, as the community begins to look for clarification, a slight new direction in lifestyle, expectations, attitudes and behaviour will have to take place.

To the West Bank Palestinian family, the day to day instability of the area is such that its future is determined by decisions made by the Israeli civilian and military authorities.

Appendix

Table I. *Problems Faced at the Beginning of Marriage by Male and Female Sub-samples*

Main problems	*Male sample*		*Female sample*	
	Frequency	*Percentage*	*Frequency*	*Percentage*
1. Problems associated with 'other' spouse (sexual, differences in age and education etc.)	75	16.6	61	12.9
2. Other human-related factors (mother-in-law, relatives, neighbours)	48	10.6	114	24.1
3. Economic hardships	110	24.3	72	15.2
4. Change in lifestyle	19	4.2	26	5.5
5. Sickness (own or other members of the family)	2	0.4	3	0.6
6. Living away from parents/children (*i.e.* original home)	11	2.4	28	5.9
7. Israeli military occupation	4	0.9	0	0.0
8. Other non-human related circumstances (difficulties in work, transportation, housing etc.)	44	9.7	12	2.5
9. No problems	128	28.3	133	28.1
10. No answer	6	1.3	18	3.8
11. Not having children	5	1.1	6	1.3

Table II. *Problems Faced During* Current *Marital Life by Male and Female Sub-samples*

Main problems	*Male sample*		*Female sample*	
	Frequency	*Percentage*	*Frequency*	*Percentage*
1. Problems associated with 'other' spouse (sexual, differences in age, education etc.)	44	9.7	36	7.6
2. Other human-related factors (mother-in-law, neighbours, relatives)	33	7.3	62	13.1
3. Economic hardships	115	25.4	81	17.1
4. Change in lifestyle	8	1.8	27	5.7
5. Sickness (own or other members of the family)	14	3.1	15	3.2
6. Living away from parents/children (*i.e.* original home)	8	1.8	3	0.6
7. Israeli military occupation	3	0.7	2	0.4
8. Other non-human related circumstances (difficulties in work, transportation, housing etc.)	20	4.4	17	3.6
9. No problem	190	42.0	199	42.1
10. No answer	11	2.4	23	4.9
11. Not having children	5	1.1	8	1.7
12. Missing value	1	0.2	0	0.0
	452		473	

Table III. *Aspects of Pre-marital Life Being Missed by Male and Female Sub-samples*

Main problems	*Males*		*Females*	
	Frequency	*Percentage*	*Frequency*	*Percentage*
1. Entertainment, hobbies, rest, furthering education	124	27.4	55	11.6
2. Being close to parents/family	4	0.9	58	11.8
3. Freedom	75	16.6	110	23.3
4. Going back to Palestine	4	0.9	11	2.3
5. Lack of responsibility	25	5.5	24	5.1
6. Do not know	1	0.2	0	0.0
7. No answer	219	48.5	216	45.7
8. Missing value	0	0.0	1	0.2
	452		475	

Table IV. *Male and Female Sub-sample Responses of Worst Features of Their Marital Life*

Main problems	Males		Females	
	Frequency	Percentage	Frequency	Percentage
1. Nothing	140	31.0	125	26.4
2. Everything	2	0.4	7	1.5
3. No answer	13	2.9	30	6.2
4. Spouse related (adjustement to marital life)	144	31.9	92	19.5
5. Changes in economic/social system	12	2.7	15	3.4
6. Alienation, boredom	24	5.3	45	9.5
7. Problems/obligation imposed from outside	7	1.5	34	7.2
8. Responsibility	28	6.2	41	8.7
9. Working (in house/job)	52	11.5	66	14.0
10. Children	1	0.2	3	0.6
11. Israeli occupation	20	4.4	3	0.6
12. Sickness (own or other members)	9	2.0	11	2.3
	452		472	

Table V. *Male and Female Sub-sample Responses of the Most Pleasant Feature of Their Marital Life*

	Males		*Females*	
	Frequency	*Percentage*	*Frequency*	*Percentage*
1. Communication/understanding spouse	156	34.5	214	45.7
2. Children	146	32.3	125	26.4
3. Nothing	20	4.4	28	5.9
4. Sex	3	0.7	3	0.6
5. Other irrelevant responses (*e.g.* listening to Arabic music)	3	0.7	5	1.1
6. Everything	12	2.7	35	7.4
7. Having responsibility	101	22.3	40	8.5
8. Being settled	8	1.8	13	2.7
9. Freedom/entertainment	1	0.2	1	0.2
10. No answer	2	0.4	9	1.9
	452		473	

Table VI. t-*test results of Frequency of Husbands Accompanying Wives When They Go Out (by three age groups)*

	All/most of the time	*Never*	*Total*
(M1) 1. Young	55	25	80
(M2) 2. Middle-age	74	30	104
(M3) 3. Old	25	8	33
			217

$f = 1.252$; $f < F\ (0.92, 2, 3) = 9.95$; $1.25 < 9.55$
Accept H_0: M1 and M2 and M3

Table VII. *Educational Level of Three Age Groups (male sub-sample)*

Part or all	*No education*		*Primary*		*Preparatory*		*Secondary*		*Tertiary*		*Post secondary diploma*	
1. Young	1	0.6%	31	17.1%	61	33.7 %	49	27.1%	17	9.4%	22	12.2%
2. Middle-age	9	4.6%	69	35.4%	32	16.46%	47	24.1%	25	12.8%	13	6.7%
3. Old	18	23.7%	33	43.4%	6	7.9%	11	14.5%	6	7.9 %	2	2.6%
Column total		6.2%		29.4%		21.9%		23.7%		10.6%		8.2%

Table VIII. *Educational Level of Three Age Groups (female sub-sample)*

Part or all	*No education*		*Primary*		*Preparatory*		*Secondary*		*Tertiary*		*Post secondary diploma*	
1. Young	13	6.4%	45	22.3%	57	28.2%	57	28.2%	11	5.4%	19	9.4%
2. Middle-age	73	31.6%	77	33.3%	32	13.9%	32	13.9%	5	2.2%	12	5.2%
3. Old	19	47.5%	14	35.0%	3	7.5%	3	7.5%	0	0.0%	1	2.5%
Column total		22.2%		28.8%		19.5%		19.5%		3.4%		6.8%

Table IX. *Residence Outside the West Bank (over one year)*

Responses	*Frequency*	*Percentages*
1. Have resided	225	24
2. Have not resided	693	75
3. No answer	6	1
4. M.V.	1	0

Table X. *Distribution of Employed Palestinian Males on the West Bank in 1977*

	Cities %	*Villages %*
1. General services	14.6	9.8
2. Trade	24.8	11.8
3. Industry/transport/construction	11.8	29.7
4. Other services	8.6	2.2
5. Agriculture	4.8	28.0

Source Abu-Lughod, J. *Demography of the Palestinians* (translated into Arabic), Jerusalem, Arab Studies Society, 1982 (p.117).

Table XI. *Person(s) who First Selected 'Wife' For Marriage (controlling for area)*

	Husband		*Wife herself*		*Bride-groom's family*		*Bride's family*		*Relations*		*Friends*		*No answer*	
1. Hebron	100	50%	0	0%	82	41%	7	4%	2	1%	6	3%	3	1%
2. Jerusalem	104	53%	12	6%	55	28%	10	5%	8	4%	5	3%	2	1%
3. Jiffna	68	51%	8	6%	34	26%	19	14%	3	2%	0	0%	1	1%
4. Khader	51	34%	2	1%	54	37%	36	25%	1	1%	1	1%	1	1%
5. Dhaisha	45	43%	13	12%	35	34%	6	6%	1	1%	0	0%	4	4%
6. Tul-Karem	55	38%	1	1%	70	49%	8	6%	6	4%	4	3%	0	0%

Table XII. *Indications by Female Sub-sample of Whether or not Spouses Verbally Communicated with Each Other Before Marriage (controlling for area)*

	Had spoken		*Had not spoken*	
1. Hebron	46	46.9%	52	53.1%
2. Jerusalem	45	45.5%	54	54.5%
3. Jiffna	35	54.7%	29	45.3%
4. Khader	28	40.6%	41	59.4%
5. Dhaisha	16	33.3%	32	66.7%
6. Tul-Karem	20	23.3%	66	76.7%
Column total	190	40.9%	274	59.1%

Table XIII. *Frequency Distribution of Number of Children per Household (controlling for area)*

	None at all		1–2 children		3–4 children		5–7 children		8–10 children	
1. Hebron	21	10.5%	33	16.5%	72	36.0%	44	22.0%	30	15.0%
2. Jerusalem	11	5.6%	19	9.6%	90	45.7%	59	29.9%	18	9.1%
3. Jiffna	1	0.7%	8	6.0%	73	54.5%	39	29.1%	13	9.7%
4. Khader	17	11.6%	12	8.2%	37	25.3%	58	39.7%	22	15.1%
5. Dhaisha	6	5.8%	10	9.6%	39	37.5%	33	31.7%	16	15.4%
6. Tul-Karem	0	0.0%	16	11.1%	33	22.9%	38	26.4%	57	39.6%
Column total		6.1%		10.6%		37.2%		29.3%		16.9%

Table XIV. *Sample Responses as to Whether Husband Accompanies Wife When he Goes Out (controlling for area)*

	All the time		*Most of the time*		*Some of the time*		*None at all*	
	Frequency	*Percentage*	*Frequency*	*Percentage*	*Frequency*	*Percentage*	*Frequency*	*Percentage*
1. Hebron	23	11.5	51	25.5	86	43.0	40	20.0
2. Jerusalem	15	7.6	52	26.4	93	47.2	37	18.8
3. Jiffna	13	9.7	39	29.1	74	55.2	8	6.0
4. Khader	27	18.5	34	23.3	69	47.3	16	11.0
5. Dhaisha	8	7.7	23	22.1	68	65.4	5	4.8
6. Tul-Karem	7	4.9	8	5.6	72	50.0	57	39.6
Column total		10.1		22.4		49.9		17.6

Table XV. *Sample Responses as to Whether Post-1967 Marital Conditions are Better Than Pre-1967 (controlling for area)*

	Post-1967, better		*Pre-1967, better*		*The same*	
1. Hebron	81	40.9%	81	40.9%	36	18.2%
2. Jerusalem	85	43.8%	77	39.7%	32	16.5%
3. Jiffna	56	42.7%	67	51.1%	8	6.1%
4. Khader	64	43.8%	69	47.3%	13	8.9%
5. Dhaisha	52	50.0%	31	29.8%	21	20.2%
6. Tul-Karem	62	44.3%	73	52.1%	5	3.6%
Column total		43.8%		43.6%		12.6%

Table XVI. *Responses to the Question: 'Do you miss any pre-marital aspects of your life?' (controlling for area)*

	Yes		*No*	
1. Hebron	98	49.7%	99	50.3%
2. Jerusalem	111	56.3%	86	43.7%
3. Jiffna	92	69.2%	41	30.8%
4. Khader	60	41.1%	86	58.9%
5. Dhaisha	54	51.9%	50	48.1%
6. Tul-Karem	71	50.4%	50	49.6%
Column total		52.9%		47.1%

Table XVII. *Aspects of Pre-marital Life Being Missed by Sample (controlling for area)*

	Don't know	*Entertainment, hobbies, rest, furthering education*		*Being close to parents, relatives, family*		*Freedom*		*Going back to Palestine*		*Lack of responsibility*		*No answer*	
		Freq.	*Percen.*	*Freq.*	*Percen.*	*Freq.*	*Percen.*	*Freq.*	*Percen.*	*Freq.*	*Percen.*	*Freq.*	*Percen.*
1. Hebron	0	38	19.0	9	4.5	40	20.0	8	4.0	6	3.0	99	49.5
2. Jerusalem	0	18	9.2	41	21.0	35	17.9	4	2.1	8	4.1	89	45.1
3. Jiffna	0	49	36.6	7	5.2	27	20.1	1	0.7	10	7.5	40	30.0
4. Khader	0	41	28.1	0	0.0	15	10.3	1	0.7	2	1.4	87	59.5
5. Dhaisha	0	9	8.9	1	1.0	30	28.8	0	0.0	14	13.5	50	48.1
6. Tul-Karem	0	24	16.7	2	1.4	38	26.4	1	0.7	9	6.3	70	48.6

Bibliography

Abu Khadra, Rihab 'Recent changes in Lebanese Muslim marriage shown by changes in marriage contracts' (unpublished M.A. thesis), Department of Sociology and Anthropology, American University of Beirut, 1959.

Abu Khadra, R. Recent changes in Lebanese Moslem marriages (unpublished thesis), American University of Beirut, March 1969.

Abu Kisbik, B. *Human settlements: Problems and social dimensions in the West Bank and Gaza Strip* (prepared for the U.N. Economic Commission for Western Asia) Bir Zeit Uni-Research Centre, November 1980.

Abu Kisbik, B. *Report on the industrial and economic trends in the West Bank and Gaza Strip* (prepared August 1981).

Abu Lughod, I. *ed. The Transformation of Palestine*, Evanston Illinois, 1971.

Abu Lughod, J. 'The demographic transformation of Palestine' in Abu Lughod, I; *ed.*, 1971.

Abu Zahra, N. 'On modesty of women in Arab Moslem villages: a reply' *American Anthropologist*, 72 (5), 1970 (pp.1079–1088).

Adams, Bert N. *Kinship in an Urban Setting*. Chicago: Markham, 1968.

Al-Akhrass, M. S. 'Structure and functions of the Arabic family' (unpublished paper), 1974.

Albrecht, J. 'Changing family and sex roles' in *Journal of Marriage and Family*, February 1979.

Al-Ibrashi, M. *Makānat al Mara fi al Islam* (The position of women in Islam), Cairo, 1971.

Allport, E. A.'The Mzab' in *Peoples and Cultures of the Middle East*, Vol. II, L. Sweet *ed.* New York, The Natural History Press, 1970 (pp.225–241).

Antoun, Richard T. 'On the modesty of women in Arab Muslim villages', *American Anthropologist*, Vol. 70 (4), 1968 (pp.671–197).

Antoun, Richard R. *Arab Village*. Bloomington: Indiana University Press, 1972.

Anum, H. *Palestinian Arabs in Israel*: Two Case Studies, London, Ithaca Press, 1977.

Appelbaum, R. *Theories of Social Change*. Chicago, 1970.

Aruri, N. *Jordan*. The Hague, M. Nijhoff, 1972.

Aruri, N. 'Palestinian emigration and Israeli land expropriation in the Occupied Territory' *Journal of Palestine Studies*, 3 (Autumn, 1975) (p.110).

Asmar, F. *To be an Arab in Israel*, London, Frances Printer, 1975.

Aswad, Barbara C. 'Key and peripheral roles of noble women in a Middle Eastern plains village' *Anthropological Quarterly*, Vol. 40, 1967 (pp.139–152).

Ata, I. W. 'Prospects and retrospects on the role of Moslem Arab women at present: trends and tendencies', in *Islamic Culture*, Vol. LV, No. 4, 1981.

Ata, I. W. 'Impact of westernization, and other factors on the changing status of Moslem women' in *The Eastern Anthropologist*, Vol. 37, No. 2, 1984 (pp.95–126).

Ayoub, M. 'Parallel cousin marriage and endogamy: a study in sociometry' *SWJA* 15, 1959 (pp.266–275).

Ayyad, M. 'The Future of Culture in Arab Society' in Laquer, W. *ed. The Middle East in Transition*, New York, 1958.

Baedecker, K. *Palestine and Syria*, Leipzig, 1912.

Baer, Gabriel *Population and Society in the Arab East*. London: Routledge and Kegan Paul, 1964 (translated by Hanna Szoke).

Barhoum, M. 'Courtship, marriage and the family in Jordan', in *Family in the Muslim World*, by Man Das *ed.*, University of Northern Illinois, Vilaas Pub. Co., 1983.

Barnett, H. 'Personal conflicts and cultural change' *Social Forces* 20, 1941 (pp.160 –171).

Barth, F. 'Fathers' brothers' daughter marriage in Kurdistan' *S.W.J.A.* 10, 1954 (pp.164–171).

Basson, P. 'Male emigration and the authority structure of families in North West Jordan' (report submitted to the Institute for Women's Studies in the Arab World) B.U.C. Beirut, January 1984.

Beck, Dorothy F. 'The changing Moslem family of the Middle East', *Marriage and Family Living*, Vol. 19, 1957 (pp.340–347).

Bendix, R. 'Traditions and modernity reconsidered' *Comparative Studies in Sociology and History*, Vol. 9, 1967 (pp.292–346).

Berelson, Bernard and Steiner, Gary A. *Human Behaviour, an Inventory of Scientific Finding*, New York, Harcourt, Brace and World, 1964.

Berger, Morroe *The Arab World Today*, Garden City, N.Y. Doubleday and Co., 1964.

Bergman, A. *Economic Growth in the Administered Areas*, 1968–1973, Jerusalem Bank of Is. Research Dept., 1975.

Bliss, Frederick J. *The Religions of Modern Syria and Palestine*, New York: Charles Scribner's Sons, 1917.

Bourdin, P. *Outline of a Theory of Practice*, Cambridge, Univ. Press, 1977.

Bruhns, F. 'A study of Arab refugee attitudes', *Middle East Journal* 9, 1955 (pp.130–38).

Bruno, M. 'Israeli policy in the administered territories', in *Israel, The Arabs and the Middle East, ed.* by Irving Home and Carl Gersham, New York, Bantan, 1972 (p.257).

Bujra, A. 'The relationship between the sexes amongst the Beduin in a town' unpublished paper delivered at the Mediterranean Social Science conference, Athens, 1966.

Bull, V. A. *The West Bank, Is It Viable*, Lexington Mass. Lexington Books, 1975.

Burckhardt, J. L. *Travels in Syria and the Holy Land*, John Murray, 1922.

Castillo, Gelia T. Weisblat, Abrahim M., Villareal and Felicidad R., 'Concepts of nuclear and extended family: an exploration of empirical referents', *International Journal of Comparative Sociology*, Vol. 9, 1968 (pp.1–40).

Chatila, Khaled *Le mariage chez les Musulmans en Syrie*, Paris: Librairie, Orientaliste Paul Geuthner, 1934.

Chomsky, N. 'Israel and the Palestinians' in Davis, U., *et. al. Israel and the Palestinian*, London, Ithaca Press, 1975.

Churchill, Charles W. *The City of Beirut: A Socio-economic Survey*. Beirut: Dar el Kitab, 1954.

Churchill, Charles W. 'An American sociologist's view of seven Arab cities', *Middle East Economic Papers*, Economics Research Institute, American University of Beirut, 1967 (pp.13–39).

Churchill, Charles W. and Sabbagh, Tony 'Beirut, two time levels', *Middle East Economic Papers*, Economics Research Institute, American University of Beirut, 1968 (pp.35–66).

Cohen, A. *Arab Border Villages*. Manchester, 1965.

Dakkak, I. *Al Quds Fi Ashr Sanawat* (Jerusalem during ten years 1967–1977) Jerusalem: Arab Forum Thought, 1981.

Daniel, N. *Islam and the West: The Making of an Image*. Edinburgh, University Press, 1960.

DeVos, G. *Responses to Change*. New York, Nostand, 1976.

Diab, L. N. and Prothro, E. T. 'Cross-cultural study of some correlates of birth order' *Psychological Reports*, 1968, 22 (pp.1137–1142).

Dodd, P. 'Women's honor in contemporary Arab society', paper presented to the section on Family Research, 7th World Congress, International Sociological Association, Varna Bulgaria, September 1970. Abstracted in *Sociological Abstracts*. Vol. 18, August 1970 (pp.785–786).

Dodd, P. C. 'Youth and women's emancipation in Egypt', in J. Landau (*ed.*) *Man State and Society in the Contemporary Middle East*. N.Y. Praeger, 1972.

Dodd, P. 'Family honor and the forces of change in Arab society', *International Journal of Middle East Studies*, Vol. 4, 1973 (pp.40–54).

Feber, M. 'Husbands, wives and careers' in *J.M. and F.*, May 1979.

Fisher, S. N. *Social Forces in the Middle East*. New York, Cornell University, 1955.

Flapan, S. 'Integrating the Arab village' *New Outlook*, 5, 1962 (pp.22–29).

Gibb, H. A. R. 'The reaction in the Middle East against western culture' in B. Rivlin and J. S. Szylowics (*eds.*), *The Contemporary Middle East and Innovation*. New York, Random House, 1965 (pp.132–140).

Goode, William J. *World Revolution and Family Patterns*. New York: Free Press, 1963. (Paperback edition 1970.)

Granqvist, Hilma *Marriage Conditions in a Palestinian Village*. Helsingfors: Societas Scientiarum Fennica, Part I, 1931; Part II, 1935.

Granqvist, Hilma *Birth and Childhood Among the Arabs*. Helsingfors: Soderstrom and Co., 1947.

Gulick, John. *Tripoli: A Modern Arab City*. Cambridge, Mass: Harvard University Press, 1967.

Gulick, J. 'Culture, change and psychological adjustment in Arab Society and the Middle East' (paper presented at the 8th Congress of Anthropological and Ethnological Sciences) Tokyo, Kyoto, September 3–10, 1968.

Gulick, John 'The Arab Levant', in *The Central Middle East*, Louise E. Sweet (*ed.*), New Haven, Connecticut, Human Relations Area Files, Vol. I, 1968 (pp.111–193).

Hacker, Jane M. *Modern Amman: A Social Study*. Durham: Durham Colleges in the University of Durham, 1960.

Hagen, Everette E. *On the Theory of Social Change*. Homewood, Illinois: Dorsey Press, 1962.

Heller, M. 'Politics and social change in the West Bank since 1967', in Migdal, J. *ed. Palestinian Society and Politics*. 1980 (pp.185–211).

Hirabayashi, Gordon and Ishaq, May 'Social change in Jordan: a quantitive approach in a non-census area', *American Journal of Sociology* Vol. 64, 1958 (pp.36–40).

Hourani, A. *Minorities in the Arab World*, London, 1947.

Hourani, A. 'A decade of revolutionary social and political changes, 1949–1969', in Kerekes, T. *The Arab Middle East and Muslim Africa*, N.Y. Praeger, 1960.

Ibrahim, Saad-Eddin 'Urbanisation in the Arab World', *Population Bullletin of the UN–ECWA*, No. 7, July 1974 (pp.74–102).

Ibrahim, S. E. *et al., ed. Arab Society in Transition*. Cairo, American University Press, 1977.

(Israeli) Co-ordinator of Government Operation in the Administered Territories. *Four Years of Military Administration, 1967–1971*, Data on Civilian Activities in Judea, and Samaria. (m.p.m.d.)

(Israeli) Central Bureau of Statistics, *Statistical Abstract of Israel*, Vol. 26, Jerusalem, 1975.

Issawi, Charles 'Growth and structural change in the Middle East', *Middle East Journal*, Vol. 25, 1971 (pp.309–324).

Jiryis, S. *The Arabs in Israel*. Beirut, Institute of Palestine Studies, 1968.
Kanana, S. *Al Tagheēr Al-Ijtimai*. Birzeit University Archives Center, 1978.
Kanovsky, E. *The Economic Impact of the Six Day War*. New York, Praeger, 1970.
Kassees, Assad S. 'Cross cultural comparative familism of a Christian Arab people', *Journal of Marriage and the Family*, Vol. 34, 1972 (pp.538–544).
Katchadorian, H. 'The mask and the face: a study of make believe in Middle Eastern Society' in *Middle East Forum*, Vol. 37, 1961 (pp.15–18).
Korson, J. Henry 'Dower and social class in an urban Moslem community' *Journal of Marriage and the Family*, Vol. 29, 1967 (pp.527–533).
Korson, J. Henry 'Student attitudes toward mate selection in a Moslem Society', *Journal of Marriage and the Family*, Vol. 31, 1969 (pp.153–165).
Landau, J. *The Arabs in Israel*. London, 1969.
Lerner, D. *The Passing of Traditional Society: Modernising the Middle East*, New York, The Free Press, 1958.
Lichtenstaedter, I. 'The Moslem woman in transition' *Sociologos*, N.S. Vol. III, Berlin, 1957.
Lowenthal, M., *et al. Four Stages in Life*. San Francisco, Jossey–Bass, 1975.
Lube, M. 'Changing behaviour and outlook of ageing male and female', in *Family Relations*, Vol. 31, January 1982 (p.147).
Lutfiyya, A. *Baytin: A Jordanian Village*. Mouton, Hague, 1966.
Lutfiyya, A. 'Islam and village culture', in A. Lutfiyya and C. W. Churchill *eds. Readings in Arab Middle Eastern Societies and Culture*. Mouton, Hague, 1970.
Maher, V. 'Social stratification and the role of women in the Middle Atlas of Morocco (unpublished Ph.D. dissertation) Cambridge University, 1972.
Mansour, A. *et al.* 'Arab Jerusalem after annexation' *New Outlook*, Vol. 14, No. 1, January 1971 (pp.28–33).
Marx, E. 'Changes in Arab refugee camps' *Jerusalem Quarterly*, Vol. 8, Summer, 1978 (pp.43–52).
Mernissi, F. *Beyond the Veil: Male and Female Dynamics in a Modern Moslem Society*. New York, J. Wiley and Sons, 1975.
Michaelson, E. and Goldschmidt, W. 'Female roles and male dominance amongst peasants' *South Western Journal of Anthropology*, Vol. 27, 1971 (pp.330–352).
Migdal, J. *Palestinian Society and Politics*. New Jersey, Princeton University Press, 1980.
Moghannam, E. T. 'Developments in the legal system of Jordan' *Middle East Journal*, VI, 2, Spring 1952 (pp.194–206).
Muhsan, H. 'Some Notes on Bedu Marriage Habits', paper presented at International Congress of Sociology', Rome 1950.

Muhyi, I. 'Women in the Arab Middle East' *Journal of Social Issues*, Vol. 15, No. 3, 1959 (pp.45–47).
Murphy, R., *et al.* 'The structure of parallel cousin marriage' *A.A.*, Vol. 61, 1959 (pp.17–26).
Murphy, R. 'Social distance and the veil' *American Anthropologist*, 66, 1964 (pp.257–274).
Nahas, M. Kamel 'Married life in Iraq' in *Studies of the Family*, N. Anderson *ed.* Tubingen, J. C. Mohr, 1956 (pp.183–219) (from *Sociological Abstracts*, 1957, No. 3825.)
Nakhleh, K. 'The goals of education for Arabs in Israel' *New Outlook*, Vol. 20, No. 3, April–May 1977 (Tel Aviv).
Nelson, C. 'Public and private politics: women in the Middle Eastern world' in *Arab Society in Transition*, by S. E. Ibrahim, *et al. ed.* Cairo, American University Press, 1977 (pp.121–130).
Nye, F. I. *et al. The Family: Its Structures and Interaction*. New York, 1973.
Othman, Ibrahim *Changing Family Structure in Urban Jordan* Mimeographed, 1974.
Palisi, B. 'Wives' statuses and husband–wife companionship' *J.M.F.* February 1977 (p.185).
Parke, R. 'Prospective changes in marriage and the family' *J.M.F.* Vol. 29, May 1967 (pp.249–252).
Pastner, C. 'Accommodation to Purdah: the female perspective' *J.M.F.* Vol. 36, May 1974 (pp.408–414),
Patai, R. 'On culture contacts and its working in modern Palestine' Memoir No 67 *American Anthropological Association*, 1947.
Patai, R. *ed. The Hashemite Kingdom of Jordan* Human Relations Area Files, 1958 (p.45).
Patai, Raphael *The Kingdom of Jordan* Princeton, Princeton University Press, 1958.
Patai, R. *Culture in Conflict on Inquiry into the Socio-cultural Problems of Israel and Their Neighbours* New York, 1961.
Patai, R. *Golden River to Golden Road: Society, Culture and Change in the Middle East* 2nd ed., Philadelphia, 1967.
Patai, Raphael *The Arab Mind* New York, Scribners, 1973.
Peretz, D. *Israel and the Palestine Arabs* Washington, 1956.
Peretz, D. *et al. A Palestine Entity* Washington, 1970.
Peristiany, Jean G. *ed. Honour and Shame: The Value of Mediterranean Society*. London, Weidenfeld and Nelson, 1965.
Peters, E. 'Consequences of the segregation of the sexes among the Arabs' (unpublished paper delivered at the Mediterranean Social Science Council Conference), Athens, 1966.
Prothro, E. T. and Diab, L. N. 'Birth order and age at marriage in the Arab Levant' *Psychological Reports*, 23, 1968 (pp.1236–1238).
Prothro, E. T. and Diab, L. N. *Changing Family Patterns in the Arab East*, Beirut, Lebanon, American University of Beirut, 1974.

Remba, O. 'Israel and the Occupied Areas, Common Market in the making' *New Middle East* Vol. 26, November 1970 (p.35).
Richardson, C. 'The Palestine Arab refugee' in *Social Forces in the Middle East*, S. Fisher, *ed.*, New York, 1955.
Rizk, Hanna 'National fertility sample survey for Jordan, 1972: the study and some findings' *Population Bulletin of the United Nations Economic and Social Office in Beirut*, No. 5, July 1973 (pp.14–31).
Rollins, B. 'Marital satisfaction' in *J.M.F.* Vol. 32, February 1970 (pp.20–28).
Rollins, B. 'Marital satisfaction' in *J.M.F.* Vol. 36, May 1974 (pp.271–).
Rosenfeld, H. 'An analysis of marriage and marriage statistics for a Moslem and Christian Arab village' in *International Archives of Ethnology*, Part II, 48, 1948.
Rosenfeld, J. 'Processes of structural change within the Arab village extended family' *American Anthropologist*, Vol. 60, 1958 (pp.1127–1139).
Rosenfeld, H. 'Changes in the occupational structure of an Arab village' *Mibphnim*, Vol. 22 (In Hebrew), 1959 (pp.71–83).
Rosenfeld, H. 'Social changes in an Arab village' *New Outlook, II* 6 and 7, 1959 (pp.37–42 and 14–25 respectively).
Rosenfeld, H. 'On determinants of the status of Arab village women' *Man*, Vol. 40, 1960 (pp.66–70).
Rosenfeld, H. 'A cultural programme for the Arab village' *New Outlook* Vol. IV, 3, 1961 (pp.36–49).
Rosenfeld, H. 'The contradictions between property kinship and power as reflected in the marriage system of an Arab village' in *Contributions to Mediterranean Sociology* J. Peristiany *ed.* The Hague, Mouton, 1968 (pp.247–260).
Rosenfeld, Henry 'From peasantry to wage labour and residual peasantry: the transformation of an Arab village' in *Peoples and Cultures of the Middle East*, Louise E. Sweet *ed.*, Garden City, N.Y., The Natural History Press, Vol. 2, 1970 (pp.143–168).
Rosenfeld, Henry 'An overview and critique of the literature on rural politics and social change' in *Rural Politics and Social Change in the Middle East* Richard Antoun and Iliya Harik *eds.*, Bloomington; Indiana University Press, 1972 (pp.45–74).
Sayigh, Rosemary 'The changing life of Arab women' *Middle East*, Vol. 8, 1968 (pp.19–23).
Schneider, H. 'Of vigilance and virgins: honour, shame and access to resources in Mediterranean societies' *Ethnology*, Vol. 10, (1), 1971 (pp.1–14).
Shamir, S. *et al.* 'The professional elite in Samaria, preliminary report' Tel Aviv (unpublished June, 1971) (pp.2–11). (Hebrew.)
Shamir, S. 'West Bank refugees between camp and society' in Migdal, J. *ed. Palestinian Society and Politics* New Jersey Princeton University Press, 1980.

Shehadeh, A. 'The Palestinian demand for peace, justice and an end to bitterness' in *New Middle East*, August 1971.
Sigelman, Lee 'Lerner's model of modernisation: a reanalysis' *Journal of Developing Areas*, Vol. 8, 1974 (pp.525–536).
Sirhan, B. 'Palestinian refugee camps in Lebanon' in *Arab Society* by S. E. Ibrahim, *op. cit.* (pp.343–359).
Speiser, E. 'Cultural factors in social dynamics in the Near East' in *Social Forces in the Middle East*, Fisher, S. *ed.*, New York,1955.
Statistical Abstracts of Israel, Jerusalem, 1969.
Stockman, I. 'Changing social values of the Palestinians: the new outlook of the Arab peasant' *New Middle East*, Vol. 9, June 1969 (pp.18–21).
Sussman, Marvin B. 'The isolated nuclear family; fact or fiction' *Social Problems*, Vol. 6, 1959 (pp.333–340).
Sweet, L. E., *ed. Peoples and Cultures of the Middle East*, Vol. II, New York, The Natural History Press, 1970.
Takla, S. 'The relationship between socio-economic class, sex role attitudes, career aspirations and internal–external orientations of daughters of working versus non-working mothers' (unpublished M.A. Thesis) Department of Social and Behavioural Sciences, American University of Beirut, 1978.
Tamari, S. 'The Palestinians in the West Bank and Gaza: the sociology of dependency', in Zureik, E. *ed. The Sociology of the Palestinians*. London, Croom Helm, 1980 (pp.84–112).
Tamari, S. 'Building other people's homes', Jerusalem, Arab Thought Forum, 1981.
Tannous, A. 'Emigration, a force of social change in an Arab village' in *Rural Sociology*, Vol. 7 (1), 1942 (pp.62–74).
Teveth, S. *The Cursed Blessing*, New York, Random House, 1970.
Tillion, Germaine *Le Harem et Les Cousins*, Paris, Editions du Seuil, 1966.
UNRWA, *Palestinian Refugees in the West Bank, Gaza Strip, Syria, Jordan and Lebanon*, January 1980.
Watad, M. 'Israel Arabs and the generation gap' *New Outlook*, Vol. 114, March 1971 (pp.25–30).
Weigert, G. *Israel's Presence in East Jerusalem* (Jerusalem, by the author, 1973).
Weingrod, A. *Israel: Group Relations in a New Society*, New York, 1965.
Weingrod, A. 'Change and stability in administered villages: the Israeli experience' in *Peoples and Cultures*, by L. Sweet, *op. cit.* (pp.124–142).
Williams, H. and Williams, J. 'The extended family as a vehicle of culture change' *Human Organisation*, Vol. 24, 1965 (pp.59–64).
Woods, C. *Culture Change*, Iowa, Brown, 1975.
Woodsmall, Ruth F. *Moslem Women Enter a New World*. London, George Allen and Unwin, 1936.
Youssef, Nadia H. 'Differential labor force participation of women in

Latin American and Middle Eastern countries: the influence of family characteristics' *Social Forces*, Vol. 51, 1972 (pp.135–153).
Zureik, E. and Nakhle, K. 'The reactivation of tradition in a post-traditional society' in *Arab Society in Transition* by S. E. Ibrahim, *ed.*, Cairo, American University Press, 1977 (pp.592–604).
Zureik, E. and Nakhle, K. *The Sociology of the Palestinians*, London, Croom Helm, 1980.

Index

MORE ABOUT KPI BOOKS

If you would like further information about books available from KPI please write to

The Marketing Department
KPI Limited
Routledge & Kegan Paul plc
11 New Fetter Lane
London EC4P 4EE

In the USA write to

The Marketing Department
KPI Limited
Routledge & Kegan Paul
29 West 35th Street
New York
NY 10001, USA

In Australia write to

The Marketing Department
KPI Limited
Routledge & Kegan Paul
c/o Methuen Law Book Company
44 Waterloo Road
North Ryde, NSW 2113
Australia

In New Zealand write to

The Marketing Department
KPI Limited
Reed Methuen Publishers Ltd.
Private Bag
39 Rawne Road
Birkenhead
Auckland 10
New Zealand

In Canada write to

The Marketing Department
KPI Limited
Methuen Publications Ltd
2330 Midland Avenue
Agincourt
Ontario M1S 1P7
Canada

This Book = a result of survey of palestinians.
Isrli Tyranny agst ~~researching~~ freely.
[Lack of freedm under Occup vi
[Isrl as 1 only democ.